KU-393-217

20 14003 750

NEW COLLEGE, SWINDON

# TALES
*from a*
# SUNBURNT
# COUNTRY

# TALES
## *from a*
# SUNBURNT
# COUNTRY

### VOLUME II

LIBRARY
WITHDRAWN
NEW COLLEGE
SWINDON

Reader's
Digest

2014003750

*Tales from a Sunburnt Country* was created by Reader's Digest (Australia) Pty. Ltd.

**Art Director:** Lena Lowe
**Copy Editor:** Lynn Cole
**Picture Researcher:** Debi Wager

**© 1999 Reader's Digest (Australia) Pty. Ltd.**
26 Waterloo Street, Surry Hills, NSW 2010
First printed in 1999.
Reprinted 1999 (twice), 2000, 2001, 2002

All rights reserved throughout the world. No part of this book may be reproduced, stored in a retrieval system, or transmitted in any form or by any means, electronic or mechanical, photocopying, recording or otherwise, without prior permission in writing from the publishers.

® Reader's Digest, The Digest, and the Pegasus logo are registered trademarks of The Reader's Digest Association Inc. of Pleasantville, New York, USA.

National Library of Australia cataloguing-in-publication data:

Tales of a sunburnt country.
ISBN 0 86449 364 9 (set)
ISBN 0 86449 366 5 (vol 2)

1. Australia – Description and travel – 1990-.
I. Reader's Digest (Australia)
919.4046

Colour separations by Rainbow Graphic Arts Co. Ltd., Hong Kong. Printed and bound by Dai Nippon Printing Company (HK) Ltd., Hong Kong

*Eucalypt grove: these Messmate stringybarks are members of an ancient genus*

# Contents

*Bunyeroo Valley in the Flinders Ranges National Park, South Australia.*

# DREAMTIME JOURNEY

By PAUL RAFFAELE

Come to tropical Arnhem Land with an
Aboriginal elder – and learn the secrets of one
of the world's oldest religions

All morning we have driven our four-wheel-drive vehicle through western Arnhem Land, some of northern Australia's roughest country. We have forded rivers where man-eating crocodiles lurk and churned our way along sandy tracks hemmed in by eucalypts and giant termite mounds. Outsiders are forbidden entry to this tropical region, 250 kilometres east of Darwin, unless they have permission from the land's traditional owners. I have been invited here by wiry, white-bearded Thompson Yulidjirri, a 65-year-old elder of the Kunwinjku people, who have inhabited Arnhem Land for tens of thousands of years.

A band of scars circles Thompson's chest, signifying his full initiation into his clan. A renowned bark painter and expert on Kunwinjku law, he is guiding me to one of the Kunwinjku's most sacred places — the home of Ngalyod, the Rainbow Serpent — to help me understand the Dreamtime.

The Dreamtime! For me, the word throbs with mystery and magic. Anthropologists Baldwin Spencer and Francis Gillen coined the term at the turn of the century as a translation of an Aboriginal expression, *altjira rama*, meaning "to see and dream eternal things." Nowadays, it's loosely used by many indigenous Australians and anthropologists to describe one of the world's oldest and most extraordinary religions.

Like many religions, the Dreamtime's tenets include gods and mortals, explain the origins of man and earth and have moral codes that regulate behaviour. But unlike many others, the Dreamtime has no written legacy like the Bible or Koran. It has at its core hundreds of "creator spirits" who set down rules for human conduct. These spirits still live within the land and influence human existence. Their rules, known collectively as the Law, have been passed down orally through generations. All creatures and humans are subject to this strict code

*Previous page:*
*A renowned bark painter and expert on Kunwinjku Law, Thompson Yulidjirri worries that the oral traditions of his people may be lost or watered down by the incursions of Western ways among his people.*

of behaviour. On rare occasions, death can be the traditional punishment for major breaches by humans. The
Dreamtime has no prayers for beseeching forgiveness
from a god – you follow the Law and prosper or you
don't and are punished.

"The Dreamtime is special in that it is based on a
belief that the land is sacred and immutable, and that
everything affecting life and human relationships
springs from it," says Kim Akerman, curator of prehistory
at the Museum and Art Gallery of the Northern Territory
in Darwin. Adds Thompson Yulidjirri, who prefers to be ad-
dressed by his first name, "Our life, our history, everything relates to the earth."

Anthropologists and Aborigines are not sure of the precise
origins of the Dreamtime beliefs, but agree they probably
began to evolve more than 40 millennia ago. Around this time,
experts say, Asians island-hopped on rafts down through the
Indonesian archipelago and landed on the northern shores of
an unoccupied great southern land. They were the first of a
wave of Australoids to settle the continent, the ancestors of
today's Aborigines. "Evidence of their life is still being un-
earthed," says Akerman. "Archaeological sites across Australia
have revealed their tools – stone-flake knives, stone pounders –
dating back 30,000 to 50,000 years."

Leaving Oenpelli, a settlement of 1000 people where our
journey began, we drive along a dusty road hemmed in by ancient granite hills and pandanus trees. Rounding a bend some
30 kilometres north of the town, a rock obelisk 100 metres
high looms suddenly against the sky.

"That's Nimbuwah," Thompson murmurs, as we walk towards the rock across the sun-baked earth. "He is a djang."
Djangs, Thompson explains, are Kunwinjku spirits who turned

*Thompson Yuli-
djirri sits quietly
beside the djang
known as Little
Brother, a pitted
stone half a metre
tall. Aborigines
believe that it is
unwise to incur
the displeasure
of any djang.*

*Thompson's tribe believe that this monolith is the form taken by the creator spirit Nimbuwah during the Dreamtime, when the gods lived on the land with the people.*

into landmarks or animals during the Dreamtime genesis after rising from godly repose in the sea. Then, the spirits lived on the land with the people, and sometimes changed into humans. Most often, though, they became prominent landforms – cliffs, mountains and watercourses – or animals or insects. "The sun and moon are also djangs," Thompson says. Traditional Aborigines have no explanation for how the sky, sea or land were formed before the creator spirits arrived, he adds. They assume they were always there and that the land originally was flat and devoid of life.

Djangs like Nimbuwah are found all over western Arnhem Land. Thompson learned the tale of Nimbuwah as a child from his father. Nimbuwah was a creator spirit travelling through the land with his wife. They were spotted by another creator spirit who soon coveted Nimbuwah's wife. "In a fight, Nimbuwah was killed when his opponent chopped off the top of his head with an axe," Thompson says, pointing to a horizontal cutting near the top of the monolith. "That's where Nimbuwah was injured in the fight before he turned to stone."

Some 100 kilometres to the east, a goanna ambles across the track. Later, we see a lean, loping dingo. "The animals are djangs, too," Thompson says. "And some of them are enemies." As an example, he tells the Dreamtime story of the dingo and kangaroo. The two were once friends. One day they painted each other's bodies for a ritual dance. The dingo told the kangaroo the parts he wanted painted but the kangaroo disobeyed him. "The dingo got very angry," Thompson says. "He told the roo he would punish him by hunting him for meat for ever. It's an example for us all. We must respect friendships."

Besides laying out a strict code of behaviour, the Law also teaches practical lessons for living; it even helps those who understand its teachings to find food. As we drive past a creek, Thompson points to several trees heavy with green, plum-like fruit. "The Law tells us that's good for curing stomach ache."

Hour after hour, Thompson relates streams of information about the birds, trees and bush foods we see. A flock of black cockatoos overhead catches his eye. "Their coming means the dry season, the premonsoonal period, will soon arrive," he says.

Thompson hopes that, having survived so long, this store of knowledge will not be lost. Although some of the young men show interest in learning the Law's lessons, the Kunwinjku beliefs may struggle to survive in the face of Western culture. "We older people can't compete with television," sighs Thompson. "Yet the creator spirits taught our ancestors that if we don't obey the Law, our world will explode."

*A disagreement between the dingo and the kangaroo over ritual body painting caused a rift between the two for all time. The story points out the values and obligations of friendship.*

Now as midday approaches, Thompson points through a maze of spiky pandanus palms to an amber-coloured hill beside a tranquil river. "That's the home of the Rainbow Serpent," he says. "Not many white people have seen it."

As we stop and peer up at the holy place, Thompson points to a spur of rock resembling the head of a dog. "That's the serpent's head," he says. "Her body is curled over the top of the rock." Suddenly he cups his hands to his mouth and begins chanting in Kunwinjku. "I told the Rainbow Serpent and other spirits that I'm bringing a

*The Rainbow Serpent, Ngalyod, like other Dreamtime deities, hears no pleas for mercy. If the Law is transgressed, the consequences are inevitable.*

*balanda* [white man] into this Dreamtime place," he says when he has finished. "If they don't approve, there'll be a flood."

Rainbow Serpent sites like this are found in many parts of Arnhem Land, often in springs, waterholes or below waterfalls. In almost all cases, according to George Chaloupka, a rock-art expert who has spent years living with western Arnhem Land Aborigines, the Serpent influences rain and causes storms and floods when people transgress the Law.

The Rainbow Serpent can punish even today. Three years ago, Thompson brought the actress Judy Davis, her husband and young son, Jack, to this spot. Thompson told them that the djang, known as Little Brother – a pitted stone half a metre high – was sacred and should not be disturbed. The family avoided the djang, but Jack broke a branch from one of the nearby trees to swipe at flies.

Disturbing a djang or surrounding vegetation can anger the Serpent, Thompson explained later. Soon after dusk, the heavens opened, though no rain had been forecast, forcing the group to abandon camp and drive through a torrential downpour. At a small village they passed through, an elder asked Thompson with a smile, "Did someone disturb the djang?"

Curiously, although dry weather is predicted all week for this area, thunderous grey clouds quickly begin to gather. I feel uneasy. *Does the Rainbow Serpent disapprove of me being here?*

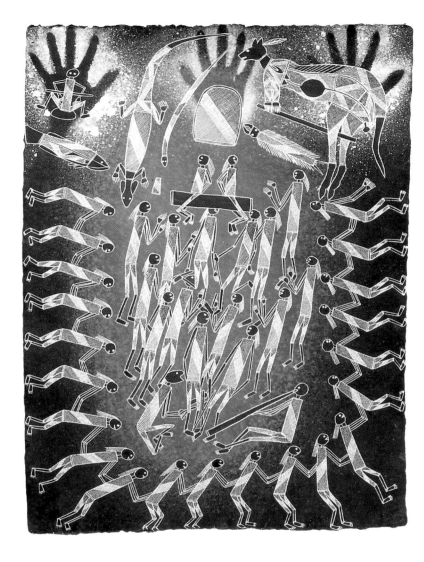

*In this depiction of a Dreamtime ceremony, an inner circle of men start to dance before the leader, who has taken the form of a kangaroo. The outer circle then joins in, to the rhythm of the didgeridoo.*

But after a few heavy drops spatter the ground, the clouds vanish and the skies are clear within an hour.

Over time, some Christian beliefs have merged with those of the Kunwinjku Dreamtime. Like many of his peers and relatives, Thompson was influenced by a mission school and now considers that there may be an omnipotent creator. "The missionaries told us that God made the land and the sky before the creator spirits came," he says, "which many believe."

Unlike traditional Christians, the Kunwinjku do not believe human life stemmed from a first couple. According to the Law, an earth mother spirit emerged, like the creator spirits, from the sea. She produced many children and carried them all over the land, leaving them in different places to procreate. As with Christians, however, Aborigines like the Kunwinjku believe in an afterlife: when a person dies, his spirit returns to settle in his father's land.

To reinforce the lessons of Dreamtime stories, the Kunwinjku regularly paint themselves with white clay and celebrate ritual dances and chants that act out the tales. They also immortalise them in bark and cave paintings. Thompson takes me to a cave about five hours' drive from Oenpelli to see some of these paintings. The cave is an overhang jutting from a sandstone rise. Panting with exertion after the climb, we enter the sudden coolness of the cavern, where a human skull wrapped in paperbark leers from a recess in the back wall. Other bones and skulls lie in the recesses. "This is the burial place of my ancestors," Thompson says quietly.

On a rock inside the cave is a red-ochre painting of a barramundi. On the rock face opposite are more pictures, some of which may have been painted thousands of years before the Egyptians built the Pyramids. Many are of animals. One picture is especially striking – a bug-eyed elf with axes attached to his elbows and feet and an extended halo joining his ankles to his hands and head.

"That's Namarrkon, Lightning Man," says Thompson. "He's a creator spirit." It does not surprise me. The Northern Territory has more lightning strikes than anywhere else in Australia. Thompson explains that Namarrkon whacks the rocks and trees with the axes to make thunder, and the halo is the lightning he produces. "When there's a storm, what we see is the tongue of Namarrkon flickering and flashing through the clouds," he explains.

Thompson moves away from me and sits cross-legged on a sloping rock, meditating on the paintings. Suddenly, he claps his hands and begins to sing in a flat, high-pitched voice. When he has finished, he explains: "I'm singing a greeting to the Lightning Man."

The Kunwinjku have close associations with all living things with which they come into regular contact. In fact, they are divided into clans named after animals. Kinga, the saltwater crocodile, features in many of Thompson's bark paintings and stories. The Kunwinjku believe the Rainbow Serpent took on the form of a giant crocodile to carve out with her body the broad muddy rivers that run down from the Arnhem Land escarpment to the sea.

As with other creatures long present in Arnhem Land, Thompson and his fellow Kunwinjku believe they must help ensure crocodiles' continued existence through Dreamtime magic. That's why he performs ritual Kinga dances and tells stories of the crocodile creator spirit to younger members of the tribe. Crocodiles are now protected, but Thompson once speared, cooked and ate the species that can reach seven metres in length, weigh more than a tonne and swallow a child whole.

As I prepare to head back to Oenpelli, Thompson clasps my hands in farewell. He will remain in his traditional land for several weeks, gaining inspiration for his paintings and visiting members of his extended family. "You now have an understanding of the Dreamtime," he says with a smile. "I hope there will always be enough people interested in our old ways to ensure that they never disappear."

# FACE TO FACE WITH THE DEVIL

By PAUL RAFFAELE

Meet one of the smelliest, greediest,
worst-tempered animals on earth

S trolling through an Australian bushland park one afternoon, I notice a pair of dark eyes glaring at me from the shade of a gum tree. A black-furred animal the size of a short-legged bull terrier stands against a wire fence. It looks like pieces of other creatures all stitched together. The front legs and sharp-clawed paws are similar to a dog's. The ears remind me of a bat's, pink and almost hairless. The whiskers are long and luxuriant, like a cat's. As I return its gaze, the animal opens prominent jaws to reveal wicked, curving canines.

Then it makes a low, throaty growl before loping away in a peculiar rocking-horse motion. I pull back as a strong stench wafts toward me. Nearly overcome, I check the sign on the fence: *Tasmanian devil*.

This encounter at the Healesville Sanctuary, 65 kilometres east of Melbourne, is my first meeting with the world's largest meat-eating marsupial. Found only in Tasmania, the Tasmanian devil has one of the most unsavoury reputations in the animal kingdom. A champion eater, the devil punctuates bloody squabbles over its daily feed of carrion and prey with the piercing screams and howls that gave it its satanic name. Given half a chance, the creature will even eat others of its kind and its own young.

*Previous page and above: Rarely seen in its natural habitat, the nocturnal Tasmanian devil usually lives with others of its kind. Quarrelsome by nature, it must fight tooth and claw from an early age for its very survival.*

"Their table manners are not what you'd find at the Ritz Hotel," says John Hamilton, director of the Tasmanian Devil Park Wildlife Rescue Centre at Port Arthur.

To many, the Tasmanian devil's beastly ways come as no surprise — thanks to Hollywood. When Warner Brothers animators were looking for a new cartoon adversary for Bugs Bunny, one of them suggested something he'd seen in a crossword puzzle — "Tasmanian devil". "Taz", a yowling, drooling tornado on legs, has since become a hit with audiences worldwide.

Real-life devils can be found in nearly 20 zoos and wildlife parks in Australia and two overseas, but few people get to see the nocturnal animal in the wild. To this end, I visit the remote northeastern corner of Tasmania where farmhand Robert Canning has agreed to guide me to a devil haunt. He picks me up at 10 p.m. in the village of Gladstone, and we are soon heading north toward Rushy Lagoon, a 26,000-hectare sheep and cattle farm.

Clouds are blowing across a pale moon as Canning finally turns his truck onto a dirt road. Then a burst of moonlight reveals an extraordinary sight. Scores of wombats — stocky, bearlike marsupials about half a metre tall — graze placidly on lush green grass. "Devil country," says the reserved bushman. "Wombats are their favourite food."

Canning stops the truck. After a few minutes, in the distance, I hear screaming — desperate, frenzied caterwauling. "Devils!" says Canning.

As we pick our way through trees, a nauseating smell assails my nose. Canning's torch illuminates bone shards and scraps of fur beside a hollow in an embankment. "That's an abandoned wombat burrow that devils have taken over," he explains.

The chorus of screams now grows louder as the track descends into a mist-shrouded valley. The shrieks rise in a bloodcurdling crescendo. As we draw closer, I hear snapping, crunching and smacking noises. When we round a bend, our torches reveal a hellish tableau — seven Tasmanian devils surrounding a disembowelled wombat. Two are playing tug-of-war with its head, their faces splattered with gore. Two others tear at the wombat's stomach.

Unbothered by our lights, they continue, gulping flesh and gnawing bones. Three smaller devils crouch a short distance away, waiting for their elders to eat their fill.

Devils' natural fare is wombats, wallabies, possums and birds. But regardless of the type of food, or whether it's dead or alive, they like a lot of it, gorging themselves when they can to ensure against lean times. According to Hobart zoologist Eric Guiler, a devil can eat a third of its own weight in about an hour. "That's like a man eating 50 steaks at a sitting," he says.

They're not picky eaters either. The devil's generic name is *Sarcophilus* (from the Greek for "flesh-loving"), but it may devour anything it stumbles across. In her University of Tasmania laboratory, zoologist Menna Jones points to jars on a shelf containing a blue tea towel, rubber thong bits and part of a leather boot. "I found them all in devil droppings," she says. "They eat anything that smells vaguely digestible."

Humans may also feature on the menu. Stories abound of people who have died in the Tasmanian bush and whose remains have been preyed upon by devils. There's no record of devils attacking a live person, but scientists do not discount the possibility that they could attack someone unconscious and unable to defend himself.

The devil has powerful jaws – strong enough for its 42 teeth to crush bones to edible bits. But despite this strength, it prefers to run rather than fight – and for good reason. "Its top speed is only seven miles an hour," Jones explains. "A dog can easily outrun a devil and kill it."

The devil's wariness and its liking for weak lambs have given it a bad name among some farmers, but not among zoologists. They say the devil performs a valuable role in clearing carrion from the bush and giving disease-bearing pests like blowflies fewer places in which to breed.

Guiler has trapped Tasmanian devils to study for 15 years. To see him at work, I accompany him on a special trip to Tasmania's sparsely populated west coast. Near the town of

Zeehan, he stops his truck by a stand of eucalyptus. He finds paw marks in soft earth beside a creek.

"Devil tracks," Guiler says. "The animals sleep all day in caves, burrows or under logs and come down here at night for water." From his truck he fetches a reinforced mesh cage. Next he unwraps a smelly chunk of beef, places it in the cage and arranges the door mechanism. We set five more traps before heading back to Zeehan.

As we approach one of the traps the next day, my heart leaps. A dark shape fills the trap entirely. "A male," says Guiler. "They're slightly bigger."

We get down on hands and knees to peer at the captive. It begins to growl.

*Handling and tagging a very angry Tasmanian devil is not a task for the faint-hearted.*

Ignoring the stench of putrefaction that emanates from the animal, Guiler thrusts his face close and begins to growl himself. Surprised, the devil quietens and stares wide-eyed at Guiler. Then it growls back, louder this time, a sound bristling with menace. When Guiler growls still louder, the devil lets out an ear-splitting scream. "Feisty bloke, isn't he?" Guiler says, grinning. "That's the way they usually warn off rivals."

Much of the devil's apparent anger is ritual display, but it can become aggressive when cornered, as Guiler learned when he was freeing one from a trap a few years ago. The animal lunged at him, fastening onto one of his fingers and gashing it badly. "If he'd got a better grip, he'd have taken it off," he says.

Placing a bag over the trap entrance, Guiler opens the door. After the devil dives into the bag, Guiler pins it by the neck through the bag, then thrusts his other hand in and punches one of the grumbling animal's ears with a tattooing machine. The tattoo will allow researchers to monitor the devil's movements. After weighing his captive, a hefty 12 kilos, Guiler frees it. He has trapped scores of devils, checking for tattoos to see how far they have roamed and examining their teeth for wear and tear. "It would be easier to examine dead devils, but cannibalism is one of their less endearing traits," he says. Ageing adults are attacked and eaten by their own kith and kin.

Everything about a devil's life is tough and brutal — even its love life. A mature male fights for a female's favours, forcing his bride to stay with him by dragging her by the scruff of the neck and guarding her night and day against rivals. Neither animal eats until the affair ends abruptly ten days later with each going its separate way.

Female devils give birth to up to 20 young from 19 to 21 days after mating. The newborns, each about 60 millimetres long, immediately set off on a crawl from the birth canal along the mother's underbelly to the pouch. There are only four nipples, to which the first newborns to reach sanctuary attach themselves. The also-rans fall off and die.

Young devils are free of their mothers' care within ten months, after which life in the wild becomes dangerous for them. More than half die in their first year, including some eaten by relatives.

At the Tasmanian Devil Park Wildlife Rescue Centre, John Hamilton and I approach a pen. My ears are assailed by a cacophony of screaming, howling and growling. A quartet of seven-month-old devils housed here with their mother are the cause of the commotion. The cubs snap at their mother's face and bite into her scarred rump.

The mother's lips appear to have been torn by her cubs. "They're demanding to be fed," says Hamilton. "It's nothing

*Four cubs can be accommodated in the pouch of this marsupial carnivore, but after ten months, they are on their own.*

out of the ordinary," he explains. "What is surprising is that the wounds never get infected."

And this is the most intriguing thing about the devil – its wondrous ability to resist infection and to heal itself. It also possesses a freakish tolerance for pain, ignoring wounds that would incapacitate most other creatures.

Nobody knows for sure how the devil survives injuries so well. Subcutaneous fat helps, oozing a protective layer over any break in the animal's skin. The devil also has an apparent ability to contract its blood vessels to minimise bleeding. In addition, Guiler believes that nature has gifted the species with a poorly developed pain centre in its brain stem and a special coagulating property in its blood.

Still, he and his colleagues have yet to unlock the secret, in part because funds for experimental research are almost nonexistent. "It's a great pity," says Guiler.

"The devil's ability to fight infection and control bleeding deserves intense scrutiny. Once we understand more about its vascular system and blood chemistry, we may be able to develop human medicines to control bleeding in surgical patients or accident victims."

Until then, this malodorous, noisy, gluttonous cannibal will remain an Australian enigma – as well as being one of nature's most fascinating creations.

# By Train
# Across
# Australia

By PAUL RAFFAELE

Step aboard the Indian Pacific for a journey along one
of the world's longest and most desolate rail routes

At 2.40 p.m. on a warm Thursday in November, a piercing whistle echoes along platform one at Sydney's Central Station. The stationmaster's voice announces over the public-address system: "Ladies and gentlemen, the Indian Pacific is about to depart." At the head of a train longer than five soccer fields, the lead locomotive shoots a plume of diesel smoke into the humid air. Slowly and smoothly, the 19 silver carriages glide from the station into the sunshine and rapidly pick up speed.

Inside, in my air-conditioned cabin, I watch the suburban stations flash past the double-glazed window and feel a swell of excitement. I am setting off on a trip on the Indian Pacific, the world's first transcontinental train linking two oceans. Over the next two-and-a-half days, I will travel, along with 386 other passengers, through three time zones 4350 kilometres to Perth, farther than the rail route from London to Istanbul. On the way we'll cross vast deserts and mountains, stop at cities and some of the most remote settlements on the planet and follow the world's longest stretch of straight rail.

A jet would take us to Perth 14 times faster, but for most passengers the destination is less important than how we'll get there. In this village on wheels we'll savour life's pleasures. An on-board staff of 24 and hundreds of support personnel along the way will work to do little else but ensure our comfort and safety. And we'll relax in style. Australian National rail recently spent $12 million transforming the Indian Pacific's interiors, creating what AN claims to be one of the world's most luxurious long-distance trains.

Soon after leaving Sydney, I join driver Ian Casey in the lead locomotive's cabin. Perched in front of a wrap-round windscreen, the cheerful 54-year-old pays little attention to the green digital figures on his computerised console; he

*Previous page: Ceaselessly traversing the continent, the Indian Pacific snakes through many different landscapes on what has become known as one of the great railway journeys of the world.*

prefers to drive the train by "feel," a knack born of 20 years' experience. "I can tell by the sound of the engines or the pull of the carriages how fast we're going or if something's wrong," Casey says.

Ahead looms the jagged outline of the Blue Mountains. This 1000-metre sandstone barrier 60 kilometres from Sydney is Australia's steepest railway gradient, rising one metre for every 33 metres the train travels. Reversing the T-shaped throttle to cut power, Casey coasts down an incline to conserve fuel, then thrusts the throttle forward to send the Indian Pacific surging up a rise. He slows to take a curve, accelerating at exactly the right moment to ensure the train leaves the bend smoothly, his face furrowed in concentration. An error in judgment here could cause passengers, crockery and baggage to fall about. Too serious an error could derail the train.

Shortly after we power over the summit, a *beeep!* echoes through the cabin. Casey looks sheepish. Since departure, he has been hitting a button on the control panel every 90 seconds. "It's a dead-man's brake," Casey explains.

If a driver is incapacitated and fails to punch the button, the buzzer sounds and the train's brakes lock automatically 60 seconds later. Casey had forgotten. "I must have been day-dreaming," he says as he presses it.

*The driver's cabin commands uninterrupted views through its wrap-round windows. The gauges on the control panel display their readings in flickering fluorescent green.*

*During each one-way journey, the huge steel water tanks under the carriage floors will be refilled five times.*

At twilight, 150 kilometres into the journey, the Indian Pacific enters a valley and pulls into the coal-mining town of Lithgow. Casey disembarks as a new driver climbs aboard. Railway regulations forbid drivers from working more than 11 hours a day.

After dinner in the 48-seat dining car, I visit Dave Goodwin, the stocky 45-year-old train manager who is running over passenger lists in an office the size of a broom closet. "I've been with the railway since I was a lad," he says. "You get used to working in confined spaces."

Until tomorrow afternoon when we reach Adelaide and another manager will take his place, Goodwin will be responsible for the crew and passengers' safety and comfort. On duty, he seldom gets more than an hour or two's sleep. On a recent trip, a man had a fatal heart attack in the dining car. Goodwin had to stop the train at an outback station and load the body into a coffin kept in the brake van. "There are always crises," he says.

Sure enough, a few minutes later a buzzer sounds above his head, alerting him to a blue light flashing in the corridor — someone signalling for help. Goodwin hurries down the corridor to seat 42 where a man in his sixties is pale and perspiring. "I had heart surgery just a few weeks ago and I can't breathe properly," he gasps.

"Don't worry, sir, some oxygen will see you right," Goodwin replies soothingly. A trained medical aide, Goodwin hurries to the dining car to fetch an oxygen cylinder. He clamps a mask on the passenger, who breathes deeply for a few minutes then says, "Thanks, I feel better."

Back in his office, Goodwin uses his mobile phone to call a train coordinator at Adelaide, hub of the Indian Pacific's operations. "Please have an ambulance at the station when we arrive," he says.

As night deepens, the Indian Pacific enters sheep country, passing hamlets with melodic Aboriginal names: Molong, Manildra, Cookamidgera. Farther up the line at Parkes, one of the two locomotives will be shut down. Nine hours from Sydney we will have crossed the last hills of any significance and one unit will be enough to haul the train to Perth.

I return to my cabin, one of nine in the carriage. A miracle of compression, it's a wood-panelled capsule three paces long and two wide. I flick a lever on the lower bunk that fits flush against the wall and doubles as a settee during the day, lowering it to form a springy bed. After folding down the fresh linen and blue doona, I tuck myself in and switch off the light. Through the window, millions of stars and the Southern Cross vault across a black sky. The sway of the train and clatter of wheels on rails quickly lull me to sleep.

Dawn is stealing over the outback when I wake and a rugged landscape now flows by the window. Glowing red dunes are dotted with dwarfish mulga trees and clumps of grey saltbush. Near the tracks I spy a trio of kangaroos.

After showering in my metre-square bathroom, I press the button summoning tea from the conductor, then visit the dining car for a traditional bush breakfast: chops, bacon, sausages, eggs and grilled tomato. At 8.45 a.m., the Indian Pacific slows as it approaches a scarred hill looming over a town of wide streets and sandstone buildings. This is Broken Hill, site of one of the world's richest lodes of silver, lead and zinc. Since ore

*The mining centre of Broken Hill, where passengers on the Indian Pacific take the opportunity to stretch their legs.*

*Every detail of passenger comfort and safety is attended to by an on-board staff of 24 plus hundreds of support personnel en route.*

was discovered here in 1883 by a boundary rider, miners have clawed out, in today's values, $50 billion worth of precious metals. I join others eager to stretch their legs along the platform, but reel back as Dave Goodwin opens the carriage door. "The air's got a sting in it today," he says. "It feels like 40 degrees Celsius already."

Despite the heat, there's no respite for Goodwin and the train's crew, whose job at Broken Hill is to take on water from underground tanks by the tracks. Goodwin steps onto the platform and drags a thick hose from a manhole, locking the nozzle into a gasket behind a panel on the carriage wall. Water flows to a steel tank under the carriage floor. From Sydney to Perth we'll refill the tanks five times.

Soon after leaving Broken Hill, the musical clickety-clack of the wheels is replaced by a gentle murmur. "The rails up to Broken Hill are held together by old-style wooden sleepers which make that distinctive sound," Goodwin explains as we sip coffee in his office. "From here to Perth they've been replaced by concrete ones." Over the past decade, five million concrete sleepers have been laid along these tracks at a cost of half-a-billion dollars to taxpayers. They're getting their money's worth, Goodwin says. A wooden sleeper lasts five years. Concrete sleepers will last more than half a century.

By midafternoon on the second day, dunes have given way to wildflowers – crimson wild hops, yellow daisies and purple Salvation Jane. As dusk approaches, the plains are replaced by red-roofed bungalows – the outer suburbs of Adelaide, where the train will pause for an hour before the 2400-kilometre haul to Perth.

At Adelaide Central, the sick passenger is helped into an ambulance while workers swarm around the train to clean carriages and refuel the loco. Coordinating the stopover is acting rolling-stock supervisor Zac Diassinas, a dark-haired man who paces the platform like a general on a battlefield, walkie-talkie to ear, barking commands. "Water tank's leaking in Carriage H," he tells a plumber. The man crawls under the train and detects a small hole in the tank. Using a blowtorch, he brazes a piece of metal over the hole in ten minutes.

Meanwhile, an examiner is checking the brakes on the train's 164 wheels with a high-powered torch. Each locomotive wheel is mounted on a solid axle and individually driven by an electric current. When the driver wants to stop the train, he hits a "dynamic" brake to cut the power, then another lever that clamps air brakes on each carriage wheel. "All clear," he radios Diassinas.

Fifteen minutes later we are on our way and are soon skirting the southwestern slopes of the Flinders Ranges, once-mighty sandstone mountains as high as the Himalayas, eroded over the past half-a-billion years to deeply pitted vermilion hills. Early in the morning, I am woken by an orange glow through the window. These are security lights from the Nurrungar tracking station, a joint Australian/American defence facility and a key link in America's early-warning system. During the Gulf War, spy satellites targeted Iraqi missiles launched at Israel and flashed the information to Nurrungar, whose scientists alerted counterparts in Tel Aviv within seconds.

Next morning, as the train slows to pass a one-bungalow settlement, six brawny men down shovels to watch us go by. These are fettlers who camp along the line. Their sole job is to maintain the train's tracks.

An unusual Landcruiser is parked by a bungalow. It has two sets of steel wheels jutting from the front and rear a metre above the regular tyres. "The steel wheels can be lowered onto the tracks," explains new train manager Greg Fisher. In the past, fettlers used hand-operated trolleys to travel along the rails. Today they are whisked along at 80 km/h by the Landcruiser.

The fettlers carry on the work of pioneers who laid the rails through this desert in the early part of the cen- tury. They faced the most daunting task of railway builders anywhere, because the desert offered no timber, food or water. To the rescue came pack camels with supplies for the rolling railway townships. Working in teams from each end of the line, railwaymen laid the tracks across 1600 kilometres of desert in just five years, finishing in 1917.

After nightfall, I notice the exit doors of each carriage have been locked. "We'll stop at several uninhabited sidings," Fisher explains. "If anyone got out for a stroll and was left behind they'd die next day from dehydration." The Indian Pacific has never lost a passenger this way, but the precaution is a reminder

that we are now entering one of Australia's dry and desolate deserts – the Nullarbor, from the Latin words meaning "no trees". The tag is highly accurate. This limestone plateau six times the size of Belgium is treeless and has little plant life.

The train drifts into a curve and then straightens for a 478-kilometre stretch of straight railway, the longest in the world. Around noon we reach Cook, an oasis of 70 people whose sole employment is to maintain tracks and provide fuel, water and medical assistance for the transcontinental trains. With typical outback humour, residents have nicknamed the settlement "Queen City of the Nullarbor". Cook consists of just

*Trees become sparse and the Flinders Ranges fade into the distance as the Indian Pacific pushes west into the vast, dry, treeless desert that is Australia's Nullarbor Plain.*

17 prefabricated houses, a hospital staffed by two missionaries, a school for two dozen children and a store. Around this clump of humanity the hot, stony landscape spreads featurelessly in all directions like a moonscape.

In stark contrast is the bright smile of Gai Didonna, missionary nurse and a Cook resident for eight years, waiting to see if any passengers need treatment. Today it's a healthy trainload. One night three years ago Didonna was warned by radio that a passenger had suffered a stroke. A Flying Doctor plane was summoned from Port Augusta. The stationmaster lit flares along the small airstrip to allow the plane to land and take the woman to hospital in Adelaide, 900 kilometres away.

*A metropolis of just 70 people, Cook's raison d'être is to supply the needs of the Indian Pacific and its passengers.*

Refuelled and rewatered, the Indian Pacific begins its final, 20-hour run to Perth. It's time for lunch. Off the main dining car, head chef Steve Balacco is scurrying about, preparing a three-course meal for some 150 people in a space the size of a domestic kitchen. Originally from Italy, Balacco has crossed the Nullarbor more than 1000 times during his 27 years of service with AN and copes expertly with the cramped facilities. "I like the job," he says, red-faced. "It's a challenge to prepare gourmet meals under these conditions." He does not exaggerate. In a single year, 220,000 meals are served on the train.

As a kitchenman removes plates from metal clamps along one wall, Balacco scoops up six steaks at a time from an electric griller, laying them alongside scalloped potatoes and broccoli microwaved a minute earlier. At great speed, the plates are passed to waiters rushing in and out. "There's little we can't prepare here," gasps Balacco. "Except cakes. The rocking of the train makes it impossible for the mixture to settle."

Indian Pacific chefs scarcely rest. After lunch, Balacco sends his assistant to the food-storage carriage for fresh supplies. He has another 432 courses to prepare by dinner and begins by dicing vegetables. On each one-way run, passengers consume 665 kilos of meat, fish and vegetables, 900 sausages, 160 dozen eggs and 100 loaves of bread.

In midafternoon, the train sways to the right as it negotiates the first bend in four hours. In the Silver City Lounge, everyone cheers. Graeme and Helen Needs, a couple in their mid-forties, clink champagne glasses. This trip is the fulfilment of a dream for the Needs. Their home in Merredin, Western Australia, is right by the railway tracks. For years they watched the Indian Pacific from their backyard, vowing to ride it across the Nullarbor one day. "It's been wonderful," says Graeme.

Foreign passengers agree. Annette Webber of Johannesburg, South Africa, and her mother, Val, flew to Australia specially to ride the train. "It's like none other," Annette says. Soon afterwards she spies a tree, her excited cry bringing other passengers to stare at the lonely mulga. It's more proof that the Indian Pacific has conquered the Nullarbor.

On and on the Indian Pacific runs, past the Kalgoorlie goldfield, reputedly the richest square kilometre of land in the world. As twilight descends over the outback, lights from isolated farm houses glimmer like beacons through the darkness.

Next morning, 65 hours after it left Sydney, the train pulls into Perth terminus with a hiss of brakes. Among the disembarking passengers, I bid farewell to new friends, regretting that the trip has ended but consoling myself with the knowledge that I have experienced one of the world's epic train journeys. Far more than a conveyance, the Indian Pacific is an adventure that retraces the heroic settling of a continent. From now on, a piece of my heart will always ride with it.

# SNAKE ATTACK!

By JIM HUTCHISON

Seven times the taipan struck, shooting murderous
doses of poison into its victim's bloodstream

C live Brady sighed with pleasure as he waded from the river. The 63-year-old railway worker was glad he had decided to swim instead of going to the races with his wife, Blanche, that August 31, 1991. A dip in the quiet, tree-shrouded Barron River in North Queensland, Australia, had been a much-loved ritual for him almost every day for 50 years.

After putting on his shoes, Brady headed home along a riverbank trail. Suddenly, he froze in midstride. One and a half metres away, a huge copper-coloured snake was gliding rapidly toward him. Brady immediately recognised its coffin-shaped head, orange eyes and creamy throat markings: the grinning death mask of the taipan.

Eleven of the world's deadliest snakes inhabit Australia, but Brady respected this one the most. Fast and ferocious when threatened, it can inject enough venom in one attack to kill within minutes. When Brady was a boy, a taipan had killed his uncle. Now, with a thrill of fright, he frantically tried to jump out of this one's way. But the 1.82-metre-long snake was too quick. Its head distended in anger, it reared and with lightning speed struck at Brady's left leg, knocking the 72-kilogram man completely off his feet.

Like a machine gun, the taipan struck seven times. At each strike, powerful muscles instantly recharged the reptile's hollow, needle-sharp fangs from glands beneath its eyes, allowing it to inject one murderous dose of venom after another. Then, abruptly, the snake swung away and slithered into the bush.

Stunned, Brady cradled his leg. Just above the knee, blood flowed from a fist-size cluster of 14 puncture wounds. Knowing that the snake's venom would be coursing through his bloodstream within minutes, Brady fought back panic. By a stroke of luck, the local hospital at Mareeba was less than a

*Previous page: Highly dangerous,* Oxyuranus scutellatus, *is found only in northeastern Australia. Its venom, often fatal, is a potent cocktail of several toxins that act on its victim's body in different ways.*

kilometre away. But to reach it, he would have to ford the river and walk up a steep trail. Shaking off the pain, he stood and began limping. How much time could he possibly have? Maybe only minutes, if he didn't get help.

Like deadly tentacles, the several different poisons in the venom shot through Brady's body. The swiftest to act was a neurotoxin that shuts out signals from the brain, attacking the eyes and then the limbs and diaphragm to cause paralysis, asphyxiation and death.

Brady began to see double. He could barely make out the trail. His legs trembled, his torso was numb, and he sucked air in laboured gasps. He had walked this trail thousands of times, but now nothing seemed familiar. *Am I going the right way?* he wondered. Suddenly, he heard voices nearby.

*Although not a commonly seen snake, the taipan is easily recognized by its coffin-shaped head, orange eyes and creamy throat markings.*

Brian Eakin, 37, a train examiner with the Queensland Railways, had come to the river with his sister Rhonda and their families for an afternoon swim. A hoarse shout made them turn round. On the far bank, a man stood swaying. "Can you help me, mate?" he called. "I've been bitten by a snake!"

"Lie down and stay where you are!" Eakin shouted. He and his 16-year-old son, Rob, waded across the river and clambered up the bank. *It's Clive Brady!* Eakin realised, recognising the man who had befriended him 17 years earlier when he'd started work with the railways. Brady's face was ashen and his eyes were vacant. "Clive, it's Brian Eakin. What happened?"

"A taipan got me," Brady wheezed. "I can't see."

"Hang on," Eakin said. "I'll get help." Instructing Rob to stay with Brady, he plunged back into the river and sprinted for Mareeba Hospital.

Nurse's aid Bernie Jo Tonon was finishing her shift when Eakin burst into the hospital. "A man's been bitten by a snake! He's down by the river," he panted. While another nurse phoned for an ambulance, Tonon grabbed a compression bandage, used to slow the spread of venom through the limbs, and headed for the river.

Excruciating cramps now seized Brady's gut. Sweat ran in rivulets down his body as he laboured to breathe. But he clung stubbornly to consciousness. *Mustn't pass out*, he told himself. *Might never wake up.*

With Eakin leading, Bernie Jo Tonon waded across the river to Brady. "An ambulance is on its way," she reassured him, wrapping his wounds tightly. "Are you sure it was a taipan?" she asked.

"I'm sure," Brady panted. "I've seen enough to know." Then, to her horror, his head lolled back and he was silent.

The petite 19-year-old struggled to turn Brady onto his side and tilt his head to clear the airway. She fumbled for the carotid pulse. It was way too fast. This was the first medical emergency she'd had to deal with on her own.

Ambulance driver Steven Qazim arrived at the scene and, together with Tonon and Brian and Rob Eakin, strapped Brady to a stretcher and carried him back across the river. As they scrambled up the bank, Brady gasped, his chest suddenly still, his lips blue. "He's stopped breathing!" cried Tonon.

"Check his pulse," Qazim replied. "If there's none, we'll have to start CPR."

While Qazim went to the ambulance to call for backup, Tonon knelt beside Brady, trying to remember what to do first. She had done CPR only on a dummy. She pulled back the man's head, gave him several quick breaths and checked his pulse. Nothing. She began pumping his chest with her hands and giving him more breaths. "Come on!" she implored, re-peating the sequence. This time Brady vomited and began to breathe again. Quickly they got the semi-conscious man into the ambulance.

At the hospital, Dr Cheryl Harnischfeger, 26, slipped a blood-pressure cuff over Brady's arm. "Eighty over 60!" The low reading meant that he was in shock and in danger of cardiac arrest. The doctor's mind raced. She knew Brady's only hope was antivenom, but she couldn't take his word that it had been a taipan. The wrong antivenom would be useless, and testing the venom to confirm the type of snake would take too long. Brady's only hope was polyvalent, a mix of antivenoms covering all poisonous Australian snakes. *We can't afford any delay*, Harnischfeger thought, setting up an intravenous drip.

Brady came to, lying on his side, doubled up in agony and retching so hard he thought his stomach was going to turn

*Blanche and Clive Brady know that luck was on Clive's side in his fight against the lethal venom of the taipan, one of the world's most deadly snakes.*

inside out. *Is this the end?* he wondered. *I should have made a will for Blanche.* He tried to force away the fog that clouded his mind.

By 5 p.m. Blanche was by his side. "You'll be okay, Clivey," she said, kissing his forehead.

"I should have gone with you to the races," her husband said weakly, trying to grin.

Slowly Brady's condition stabilised. He was rushed to Cairns Base Hospital, an hour away, where the venom in his blood was positively identified as taipan. There, he seemed to improve. But the taipan was not finished with him yet. As the neurotoxin was neutralized by the antivenom, a second insidious component of the venom began a devastating strike.

At eight o'clock that evening, a nurse taking a blood sample noticed blood trickling from the puncture when she withdrew the needle. Concerned, she called one of the doctors on duty,

Sean Newell, who hurried to Brady's bedside. Bleeding so long after the snakebite could be caused by only one thing: an ingredient in the venom that interferes with the blood's clotting mechanism. Unchecked, it could cause Brady to bleed to death internally.

Newell was shocked to see the crimson trickle of blood seeping from all 14 of Brady's puncture marks. It was the consistency of water. He looked inside Brady's mouth. Blood was dripping from his gums and puddling under his tongue.

"He needs more antivenom now!" Newell said. Then he reassured his patient: "Clive, we're going to get your clotting factor back." The doctor wished he felt as confident as he sounded. Lab tests showed that Brady's clotting factor was so low it was unrecordable.

Newell set up one drip of antivenom and another of plasma to try and stem the bleeding. For hours, however, it continued unabated. Brady's sheets were stained with deep red patches. "He won't last much longer like this," Newell said quietly. "It's amazing he hasn't had a brain haemorrhage."

By 11 p.m. Brady's clotting factor had begun creeping up. Gradually, the bleeding slowed. After 15 hours of fighting for life, Brady drifted into a deep sleep.

Clive Brady was one of the lucky ones, the survivor of a snake whose venom is nearly eight times more lethal than that of the deadly cobra. "It was a near thing," said Dr Newell, "but Brady's will to live helped him to pull through."

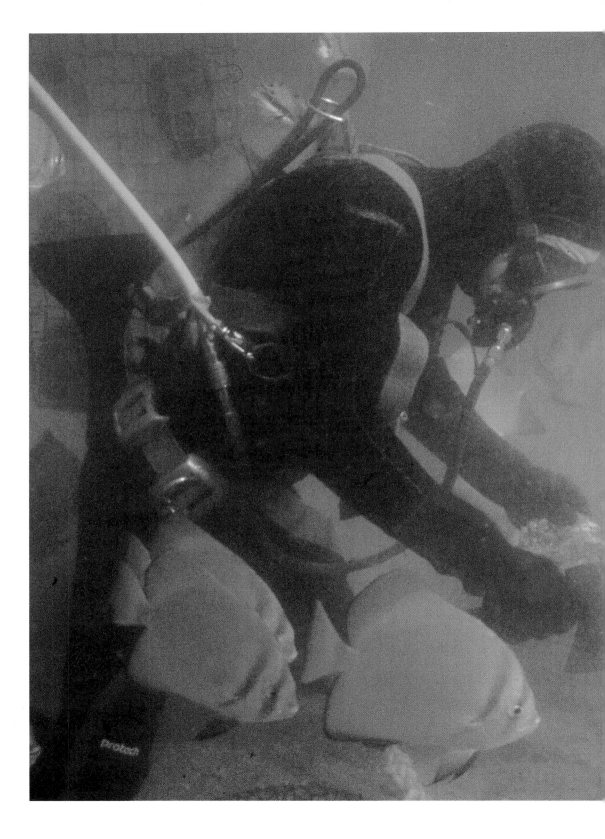

# In Search
# of the Perfect
# Pearl

By PAUL RAFFAELE

The warm tropical seas off northwestern Australia
are home to some of the most coveted
jewels in the world

To a swirl of music, a tall, dark-haired model glides down the grand staircase of the Regent Hotel in Hong Kong. Heads turn as the young woman sashays among guests at an exclusive cocktail party, and all eyes are fixed on a string of pale, marble-sized gems that encircle her neck. Against the model's golden-brown skin, the 27 silvery stones glow like little moons in the light from the chandeliers. This party precedes the annual auction of Australian South Sea pearls. Many thousands of cultured pearls will go under the hammer tonight, but this strand has attracted the most interest among the 180 international buyers and traders.

Mingling with the guests is Nick Paspaley, 47, head of the Darwin-based Paspaley Pearling Company. "These gems are real beauties," he says to a jeweller. "They are perfectly graduated in size and of fantastic colour – it took us about three years to match them." A Hong Kong jeweller has already made Paspaley an offer that is not matched in the auction that follows – one million dollars.

Pearls! Ever since the first fishermen spied these magical creations folded in oysters, they have been admired and desired as symbols of beauty, power and love. In the Bible, Christ acknowledges their worth when he uses "throwing pearls before

*Previous page: Panels of giant pearl-bearing oysters rest on the floor of the ocean as the pearls grow slowly within them. Divers clean their shells regularly to maintain the precious molluscs in peak condition.*

swine" as an analogy to warn against wasted effort. In the reign of Queen Elizabeth I, a British nobleman ground to dust a pearl worth £15,000, then mixed it with wine and drank it as a toast to his sovereign.

Pearls are commonplace today thanks to mass-farming techniques, but in the global gem trade, one type, the Australian South Sea pearl, outshines all others. Plucked from giant oysters in tropical waters off northwestern Australia, they fuel

*A panel of newly seeded oysters is returned to the ocean where the introduced irritant will become coated with layer upon layer of nacre.*

an industry that has grown six-fold in the past decade, earning Western Australia more than $200 million in export revenue in 1996 alone.

Treasured for their colour and size by celebrity collectors, including Queen Elizabeth and actress Elizabeth Taylor, these gems can be as dazzling as their bivalve creators are non-descript. A single pearl kept in Darwin is so large and translucent that it has been described by its owner as priceless. "South Sea pearls are superior, like a Ferrari is superior to a bicycle," explains Richard Torrey, Phoenix-based editor of the international newsletter *Pearl World*.

To see the birthplace of this prince of pearls, come to Eighty Mile Beach, 200 kilometres southwest of Broome in Australia's far northwest. Eight kilometres offshore, a pearling lugger rolls in the swell as the sun rises over the turquoise waters of the Indian Ocean. On board, 28-year-old diver Mick Espe hangs a string bag round his neck, preparing to enter the water for an oyster hunt along the seabed – the first step in the pearl-production process that can take three years. "Time to go shopping," Espe jokes.

Espe slips over the side and fins toward the bottom, 12 metres down. Breathing through an air hose, he peers through clouds of plankton that cut his visibility to three metres. Here, *Pinctada maxima*, the oyster that plays host to South Sea pearls, gorges on a stew of plankton filtered from the ocean. *Maxima* is found in tropical seas from Myanmar (formerly Burma) down to Australia, but it's in these waters that it grows largest – up to three kilos – and so creates pearls twice the diameter of any others.

*There!* Sitting on the seabed, Espe spots a plate-sized protrusion like a fossilised omelette. A silvery thread along one edge betrays the oyster's lips, opened to draw in food. They snap shut belatedly as Espe pulls it from its gritty limestone home and drops it into his bag. Half an hour later, deckhands haul the bag aboard and sort the shells, returning to the sea a handful smaller than 120 millimetres in diameter, the minimum legal size. The rest are stacked in a seawater tank on deck.

By dusk, Espe has collected more than 300 oysters, which are anchored in panels along the seabed. They will remain there for three months to recover from the shock of capture. Despite their dull appearance these molluscs are complex creatures. "If you run cattle you'd be a fool to treat them roughly," says Bill Reed, a marine biologist based in Broome. "The oyster's an animal, just the same."

Yet the oyster is the only creature that can manufacture a jewel. In the wild, this happens very rarely. It could take 100,000 oysters to produce one good pearl necklace. When an irritant, such as a grain of sand, is swept into the oyster's shell by a current and lodges in its flesh, the animal fights back,

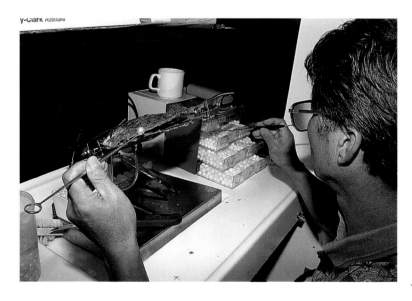

*Two-and-a-half years after the oyster is seeded, a technician plucks out a lustrous fully formed pearl.*

neutralising the intruder by coating it with a microthin layer of nacre, a silvery substance that is about 90 per cent calcium carbonate. The oyster patiently continues to lacquer the irritant, layer by layer, forming a pearl. In the vast majority of cases, this

natural gem is irregularly shaped, like the irritant, or blemished. Natural, perfectly round pearls are rarer still. "A gem-quality pearl in the wild is a freak of nature," says Reed.

To overcome these odds, Kokichi Mikimoto, a Japanese pearl trader who dreamed of mass-producing pearls so that every woman could afford a strand, realised in the late 1880s that man needed to cheat. He began to test artificial irritants in small oysters in Japan. Finally, in 1914, he stumbled on the solution: an irritant must be placed on a graft

*The harvest is in full swing and Paspaleys' daily haul of some 3000 pearls is coming together.*

of epithelial membrane from a sacrificial oyster. Without this membrane, inexplicably, the host would not co-operate. By the time he died in the mid-1950s, Mikimoto's pearl farms held more than 20 million cultured pearls and his seeding techniques had become standard practice.

To witness this next, most crucial step in the production of pearl, I visit Paspaley Pearling Company's mother ship, *Paspaley III*, anchored off Eighty Mile Beach. Australian pearl seeding and harvesting is done aboard ships, because the quicker oysters are returned to the sea, the less likely they are to die prematurely. Oysters can be used up to three times to produce gems before they die at the age of eight to ten.

After a sweltering night, I rise before dawn to join master

seeder Takenobu Hamaguchi to watch the rarely seen seeding process. Like most pearl seeders in Australia, where local expertise is still scarce, Hamaguchi was born and trained in Japan. The sky is still dark when the 30-year-old pads out onto the enclosed deck.

Sitting at his spotless operating table, Hamaguchi takes an oyster, secures it horizontally in a steel clamp at eye-level and uses a light on a stand to peer between the lips, held open by a wedge of yellow plastic. Looking over his shoulder, I notice sea water speckling the creature's innards — blobs of faint-pink tissue bordered by glistening black membrane. Carefully reaching in with a scalpel, Hamaguchi scores a nick in the gonad toward the back of the shell and uses a probe to push the minuscule folds of flesh apart.

Then, with tweezers, he lifts from a dish a thread-like strip of membrane from another oyster. Cautiously he manoeuvres the strip into the cut. Then he reaches toward a set of doll-sized drawers on his bench. These hold the nuclei, the tiny

*In an innovative move, Nick Paspaley sought to reduce stress on the oysters by carrying out the high-tech seeding and harvesting operations at sea — where the animals live.*

*When complete, this necklace of perfectly matched, perfectly round, marble-sized pearls will be sold for hundreds of thousands of dollars.*

spherical irritants made from the shell of American freshwater mussels. The nuclei vary in size from six to nine millimetres. "If I pick too big a nucleus, the oyster might spit it out," Hamaguchi says as he picks up a bead with tweezers. "If it's too small, I limit the size of the pearl." He presses the irritant into the implanted mantle, and returns the oyster to a tank. Throughout the day, he implants nuclei into 500 more.

Over the next ten days, 50,000 oysters will be seeded on *Paspaley III* before she sails for a pearl farm 400 kilometres to the north. There the jewels will grow for up to two-and-a-half years inside them. The success rate: about 50 per cent. When these pearls are eventually harvested they will fetch millions of dollars.

To prevent a ruinous plunder, the West Australian government slaps a yearly quota on the collection of wild oysters – 622,000 in 1996, of which 420,000 divided among seven licensees will be taken from the seabed at Eighty Mile Beach. More than 60 per cent of the shells are allocated to Nick Paspaley, who dominates the trade. In 1995, Paspaleys produced more than 300,000 pearls.

The final step in the pearl-production process is the harvest, this time in the coastal waters around the tropical port of Broome.

Bruce Farley, a lanky former Australian spearfishing champion, runs a pearl farm here in a joint venture with Paspaley in

Roebuck Bay. I meet him at sunrise one morning and we are soon scudding across the bay in a speedboat to board *Clare*, a purpose-built pearl-farming vessel. A harvest is in full swing aboard *Clare*, with divers hauling panels of oysters onto the deck. I stand next to Tokio Hamaguchi, uncle of Takenobu and a veteran pearl harvester, as he places an oyster in a clamp on a table. For the first time, I am about to see this miracle of nature plucked from its maker.

Tokio peers into the wedged-open oyster, then reaches into the shell with tweezers, rotates his fingers and, deftly, like a magician, withdraws a pearl that he holds up for me to inspect. The marble-sized bead is white and gleaming in the sunlight. "Medium size – about 14 millimetres in diameter," Hamaguchi says. He hands it to me and I roll it in my palm. It has a warm, silky texture.

After each pearl extraction, Hamaguchi examines the oysters carefully. Those with holes in their shells have been attacked by boring sponges or worms. He chops these in half with a machete and stacks them. Mother-of-pearl still fetches up to $10,000 a tonne from European firms using it to make buttons and inlays in jewellery. The oyster's adductor muscle, viewed as an aphrodisiac in some parts of Asia, will be dried and sold for up to $350 a kilo. The healthy oysters will be re-seeded and returned to the sea, producing a bigger pearl, because as the shell grows it can be seeded with a bigger nucleus.

Most of the harvest of 3000-odd pearls spread on a towel in the *Clare*'s mess at the end of the day are white – the kind most desired by jewellers – but some are tinted gold, pink or blue. No one knows what stimulates an oyster to produce the different colours. "It's likely that genetics play a part, but it probably also has something to do with the temperature of the sea water," says Farley.

What distinguishes a great pearl? "Look," says Farley, handing me a thumbnail-sized gem. "This one's inferior." It looks good to me as I hold it up, and I say so, but Farley shakes his head. "The surface is foggy." Then Farley hands me another and says: "This is the best we've collected today." I spot the difference immediately. This pearl's surface is crystal clear, reflecting my face. "That could fetch about $20,000," Farley says.

From time to time, an oyster will inexplicably offer up an enormous pearl. During a harvest seven years ago, Tokio Hamaguchi was incredulous when he withdrew a gem the size of a small plum. "I knew immediately that this was the pearl of pearls," he says. Knowing Nick Paspaley had an obsession about collecting unusual and oversize stones, he excitedly radioed his employer. The 21-millimetre monster is now housed in Paspaley's private collection.

The only son of a Greek migrant, Paspaley has been a major force in the creation of the modern Australian pearl business. Until the early 1980s, sales of pearls were in the doldrums. Death rates of roughly handled oysters were high, cutting profits. Japanese buyers dominated the trade and producers offered strands that were often mismatched, souring the gem's reputation. Breaking tradition, Paspaley sent his boats to the oysters to reduce stress, imposed strict standards on grading and matching, and internationalised the industry by organising the first Australian South Sea pearl auction in 1989.

In his spare time, Paspaley constantly adds to his personal collection. To become one of the select few to see it, I visit him at a Darwin address. He reaches into a safe and produces a small chamois bag. As he pours the contents onto a table, I catch my breath. The pale, perfectly round gems are each up to 20 millimetres in diameter and glowing against the dark glass of the tabletop. "This set's worth hundreds of thousands of dollars," Paspaley says.

Where, I ask, is the biggest pearl of them all – the one Hamaguchi found? Paspaley hesitates, then walks to the safe and takes out another, smaller pouch. "This is the full moon that rose over my life," he says, smiling.

He drops into my hand a huge, round, white pearl that seems astir with life, with a dancing, glittering sheen like quicksilver. As I stare into it, I see my face and the room behind me reflected below the surface, a startling three-dimensional image plumbing the layers of nacre. For a minute I am a ma- haraja, an emperor, the world's richest man as I marvel at its beauty.

Reluctantly I hand it back. Then Paspaley says, "My dream is to create the world's most perfect strand of pearls, with this one as the centrepiece." From the millions of South Sea pearls his company will harvest over the next decade, Paspaley ex- plains, he will select the very best, each rare and special in its own right, to join this huge bead in a strand he expects to sell at somewhere between $5 million and $10 million. "When I'm finally ready to sell that necklace," he says, "it will make some lucky person very, very happy."

*Nick Paspaley gazes in wonder at one of the outstanding pearls in his special private collection.*

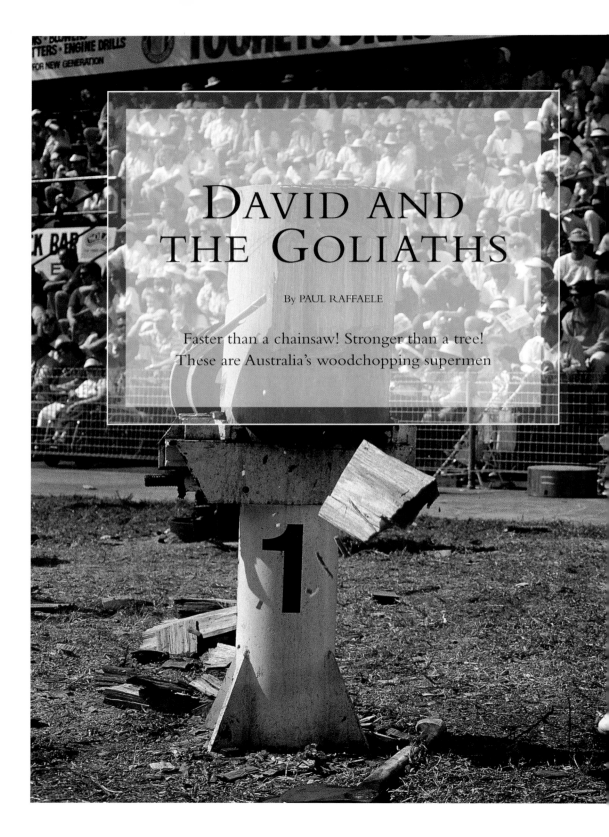

# DAVID AND
# THE GOLIATHS

By PAUL RAFFAELE

Faster than a chainsaw! Stronger than a tree!
These are Australia's woodchopping supermen

"Axemen stand to your logs," the ring announcer's voice booms across an arena in Tasmania. Eight heavily muscled men approach the 300-millimetre-thick logs in front of them. Each holds a racing axe, a perfectly balanced tool with a head polished to a mirror finish. The cheering crowd falls silent.

"One!" The thud of steel on wood echoes across the ring as one man begins chopping. "Three...four..." The announcer calls off the seconds as the others wait for their time-handicaps to expire. "Nine...ten..." Another axeman begins chopping, then another. After 30 seconds, all are thrashing away, except David Foster, a giant of a man with a chest as broad as a beer barrel. He stands impassive as the counting continues. The crowd roars its frustration. The other men have sliced deep into their wood, and the odds against Foster are overwhelming. "...Thirty-nine...forty!"

Suddenly the big man explodes into action. Thock! Thock! Thock! His axe dissolves into a smear of silver. Woodchips sing through the air like bullets as his mighty blows gouge deep into the log, first on the left, then the middle, then on the right. But the leading man is already within a thumb's width of cutting through. Foster, grunting like a buffalo, rains down three more huge blows. The crowd, ecstatic, leaps to its feet. With a final, mammoth swipe, Foster sends the top half of his log spiralling in the grass. Triumphantly he thrusts his axe high, his great chest heaving.

Woodchopping is one of the best-kept secrets of international sport, a thrilling combination of strength, precision and nail-biting suspense. Its champions, like 36-year-old Foster, are so powerful they can sever a 375-millimetre-thick log in 30 seconds, and so accurate they can split a match lengthways with one swing of their axe. Most refreshing of all,

*Previous page: Clad in regulation white strides and singlet, David Foster shapes up to his log. Each year, more than 2000 registered competitors take part in wood-chopping competitions throughout Australia.*

there are few inflated egos. "This is sport at its best," says Denzil Munday, president of the Australian Axemen's Association. "No tantrums, no steroids, just superb fitness and skill."

On any weekend of the year, you'll find a woodchop somewhere in Australia, with competitors ranging from seven-year-olds to a veteran just turned 90. "We have more than 2000 registered competitors and thousands more who take part just for the fun of it," says Munday. The holy of holies for axemen is the annual Sydney Royal Easter Show, the Wimbledon of woodchopping, where more than 2500 spectators crowd a

*Precious seconds are lost if the blade strikes the wood at the wrong angle or in the wrong place — the top axemen practise daily to hone their skills.*

purpose-built arena to see the world's best battle it out. Foster's arch rival is Bruce Winkel, a stocky, 28-year-old Queensland farmer. The previous year, Winkel had grabbed the standing-cut title from Foster. The Tasmanian had immediately set himself a punishing training program to win it back.

On a property at Latrobe in north-western Tasmania, I watch Foster start the first of two daily 90-minute training sessions. In a large tin shed hung with battle-scarred racing axes and wicked-looking two-handled racing saws, I join Foster and his son, Stephen, aged nine. "Right, let's go!" says Foster cheerily, plucking a 32-kilogram log from a pile and bolting it securely in a steel cradle. Next, Foster reaches, not for an axe, but a sledgehammer. He raises the 6.4 kilograms of steel over his head and brings it crashing down on the log.

Bang! Splinters fly. Bang! The roof shakes and the concrete floor trembles. Bang! Bang! Bang! Again and again he flails at the log, delivering 150 blows in as many seconds.

Foster, who is 193 centimetres tall and weighs 145 kilograms, uses the hammer to increase his already massive strength and endurance. But to develop accuracy, he turns to one of his racing axes. Panting from the exertion, he places a match on a log, then swings down his axe, splitting the match neatly down the middle. He repeats the feat three times without missing. "Accuracy is vital," he explains. "You've got to hit the right spot, at exactly 45 degrees – more, and you'll bury the axe in the log; less, and it will glance off." One bad stroke can lose a contest.

Foster has been swinging an axe since the age of two, when his father gave him a rubber-headed axe as a toy. At six, the boy was clearing scrub timber; by his mid-teens, he was competing at woodchops around Tasmania. "You can never be a good winner until you prove you are a good loser," his father often told him. But Foster didn't get much practice at losing. At 19, the young giant won his first major title at the Melbourne Show. In the next 15 years, he captured every major title in Australia, and in 1985 he waltzed away with the overall trophy at the Lumberjack World Championships in the United States.

Stephen looks like being a chip off the old block. "He's coming along nicely," smiles Foster and hands me an axe. "See if you can beat him." I remember being a dab hand chopping firewood in my teens. Go on, I tell myself. He's only a child.

Foster bolts two smallish logs into their cradles, and the boy and I stand with our axes resting on the logs. "Ready...," says Foster. "Go!" There is a satisfying thud as my first blow lands and gouges out a sizeable chip of wood. This'll be a push-over, I tell myself. But my second blow bites too deep, and I waste precious seconds wresting the head free. My next is too flat, and the axe skids off the wood. In the background I hear the regular, measured thud of Stephen's axe.

I continue to hack away, but I am near exhaustion. Blisters balloon at the base of my fingers. You're being beaten by a child, I goad myself.

With renewed intensity I swing and slash. But Stephen is through. "Done!" he yells. His time: eight minutes. I have cut through barely a third of my log. Foster gives his son a proud grin, then sets up a similar-sized log for himself. He demolishes it in 14 seconds.

The sport of woodchopping is said to have begun not far from Foster's home in the late 19th century. Sawyers and axe-men were in great demand all over Australia then, toppling trees to clear the bush for grazing land or for the millions of railway sleepers stringing together the colony's new cities. Proud of their prowess, these toughest of men turned their livelihood into a sporting contest.

The first recorded match took place in 1870 at Sprent, near Ulverstone, when Jack Biggs took on Joe Smith for, according to legend, a wager of 5000 palings. A two-day woodchopping carnival was staged 21 years later at Latrobe, ten kilometres down the road from Foster's training shed.

Since then, Tasmanians have been at the forefront of the sport, and Foster is constantly waylaid by well-wishers in the streets of local country towns. But he doesn't take the affection for granted. "You've got to give something back," he says.

In the playground of a primary school in Keilor, Victoria, he asks 200 excited kids to count the blows it takes to demolish a log. His axe swings down. "ONE!" yell the kids. He attacks the log again. "TWO!" the kids scream. It takes Foster just 19 blows to knock the top off the log. When the cheering dies down, he tells his young fans, "I got my strength from eating the right food, keeping fit and never taking any kind of

*David Foster watches as his son goes through his paces. Stephen already looks like being a chip off the old block.*

drugs. If anyone offers you drugs, please say no." As he leaves, the gentle giant is mobbed by children pleading for his autograph, and feeling his massive biceps.

Three months before the Sydney show, Foster has noticeably upped his cutting rate. But Winkel has been working out on his farm near Brisbane, some 1700 kilometres to the north. A dairy farmer by day, Winkel trains each night under a spotlight, chopping the same size block that the two will face when they meet in Sydney.

The fateful logs will come from one of 350 hardwood trees, designated by the New South Wales Forestry Commission and felled especially for the Royal Agricultural Society, from regrowth forest in the foothills of the south coast. "It's the best hardwood going, a proper test for champions," says forester Jim Harris, who has set aside two weeks in February to carve up the trees. Harris is himself a famed axeman, lean and stringy as the wood he topples, and he's relishing the contest ahead. "It's going to be a great tussle," he says. "Winkel's got a slight edge in accuracy, but Foster can even it up with sheer power." After inspecting the base of each tree, he chooses a mighty silvertop ash for its even grain and the tightness of its rings. After cutting the tree down, he punches the event number into the freshly cut surface of each log so every axeman in the final has wood from the same tree.

With only weeks to go before the contest, Foster takes delivery of a heavy package from Eddie Fawcett, a New Zealander who devotes his life to making the perfect axe. "He's getting pretty close," smiles Foster, cradling one of Fawcett's gleaming blades in his hands. Next to a standard axehead, Fawcett's blades are like diamonds versus paste. Champion axemen gladly pay $250 for each hand-tempered blade because of the way it holds its sharpness. "The characteristics come from the special way we treat the blades after they've been forged," says Fawcett, a brown-haired 55-year-old who has made axe heads in his tiny Masterton factory for 20 years. Each blade is heated, cooled, quenched in oil and brine and then reheated twice to emerge a last time as tough as a blade can be.

Fawcett knows the wood Harris chooses for the Sydney show is the hardest used anywhere, and he has armed Foster's four blades with an edge so keen they will shave hair. Foster, like most champion axemen, shapes his own handles to the individual contours of his hands.

It's the day of the grand final. Jim Harris wakes at sunrise in his bunk by the woodchop arena. He turns off the sprinklers that have been playing over the sawdust-packed wood since it was first cut and carts the lathe-trimmed logs into the arena, stacking them in the order of the day's events.

By mid-morning the banks of seats are packed with spectators. Most axemen are yarning with old mates as they wait for their events in the narrow dressing room beneath one of the concrete stands. But Bruce Winkel, clad in regulation white strides and singlet top, sits silently polishing his axes, his mind focused on the struggle ahead.

At the other end of the room, Foster is mulling over a painful dilemma. He is due to compete in a sawing event just three hours before his clash with Winkel. The year before, Foster and his brother Peter won the two-handed saw world championship, cutting through a 600-millimetre log in 18.44 seconds. Now they are due for a rematch. "Pull out," a friend urges him, "or Winkel will have you on toast."

But Foster can't let Peter down. They are up against New Zealander David Bolstad and Carson Bosworth, a star performer on the North American lumberjack circuit. The Tasmanians, who have beaten chainsaws in the past, rip through their 600–millimetre log in just 17.72 seconds – a new world record. "You guys are the best," says Bosworth. Foster shakes the American's hand warmly. But in his shoulder he feels the smouldering pain of a pulled muscle.

Soon after lunch, Foster, Winkel and six of the world's other top axemen gather to draw numbered marbles from a blue pouch held by a judge. The Fosters gather round the log, Peter bolting it into the cradle as his brother seeks out the soft side. Trees tend to grow quicker on the side that catches the morning sun, and the rings on that side are wider and softer. As everyone but the axemen withdraws to the sidelines, Foster slides his chosen axe from among six in a specially built carrying case. The blade is honed to a paper-thin edge.

*Brothers David and Peter Foster hold a world record for ripping through a 600-millimetre log with a two-handed saw in just 17.72 seconds.*

"Stand to your logs!" orders the announcer. The eight men fix their eyes and draw back their axes. The moment has come.

This is the world championship, and there is no handicap. The first stroke is timed for the count of three. The ground shudders as eight axes hit home simultaneously. Huge chips fly in all directions, slamming into the fence, crashing into the bodies of the two judges bravely seated nearby.

The axemen daren't look away from their logs long enough to see who is ahead. Winkel, cutting fiercely, takes a quick lead. "Dig in, David, you're behind," Peter shouts. Steeling himself

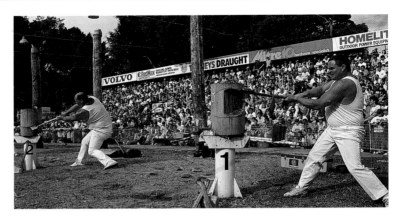

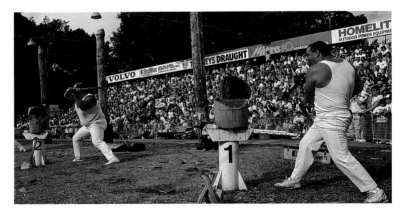

*Slashing away at logs that have been carefully selected for the competition, Bruce Winkel, right, and David Foster have no time to check on each other's progress – the heavy blows that send the chips flying must above all be accurate.*

against the pain in his shoulder, Foster quickens his blows, and his sheer power begins to tell. With his log almost severed, Foster raises his axe for a final massive stroke. Bang! The axe bites deep. But it fails to cut through. In the split second it takes Foster to yank it out, Winkel slams home his last blow. As the Queenslander's log cartwheels to the ground, the crowd erupts and Winkel raises his arms in triumph.

At a presentation later, Foster is named the show's Champion of Champions for winning three of the five world titles on offer. But he would swap them all for the one he lost to Winkel. Mindful of his father's urgings years before, Foster is generous in defeat. "Winkel won fairly," he says as he packs his

axes away. But on the plane back to Tasmania, he is already planning a training schedule that he's convinced will clinch the next encounter with Winkel.

Next morning, Foster's training shed reverberates again to the thunderous blows of his sledgehammer. "It'll be my turn next year," he says. "No worries about that."

*Victorious, Bruce Winkel raises his arms in triumph as he retains his standing-cut title.*

# THE EMU LAYS A GOLDEN EGG

By TONY MAGUIRE

Bird–brain? Maybe. But this roadrunner
of the outback has a glittering future

Driving down a quiet road in the New South Wales outback, dodging potholes, I have a strange, unaccountable feeling that I am being watched. I daren't look away from the road, but from the corner of my eye I can just see a grey shape in the bush alongside, shadowing my car. I risk a quick glance to my right and blink in disbelief. A bird as tall as a man is running alongside me. A wild emu! Suddenly the animal turns and disappears into the spring grass in a plume of dust.

This roadrunner of the outback is one of the world's most remarkable creatures. It can't fly, but it will rocket along the ground at up to 50 kilometres an hour for short bursts and then cruise at 35 to 40 kilometres an hour for ten minutes or more. When cornered, it can deliver a sledgehammer kick to deter predators. And it's a tough old bird: most other animals seek shelter from Australia's heat, feeding at dawn or dusk, but the emu will forage all day in temperatures of more than 40 degrees Celsius if they have to.

"You'll find these birds in every region of the mainland, from the lower Snowy Mountains to the hot, dry plains," says Gary Fry, keeper of the emus at Sydney's Taronga Zoo. "Emus are superb survivors."

Fry doesn't overstate. While its New Zealand relative, the moa, was hunted to extinction and its African cousin, the ostrich, was eventually saved and domesticated by farmers for its feathers, the emu has flourished even in the face of deliberate attempts to reduce its numbers. Since early last century, farmers in some areas have shot the crop-wrecking birds on sight. After a long, hot summer in 1932, wheat farmers in Western Australia called in the Royal Australian Artillery to deal with the birds. However, the emus were so quick that the diggers' 500-rounds-a-minute Lewis guns seldom found their mark.

*Previous page: Although partial to young crops and greens, the emu can eat almost anything — dry leaves, twigs, even bark, which gives it an extraordinary capacity to survive in harsh conditions.*

Although its movements in some areas still need to be controlled, the emu is today undergoing a renaissance, being raised for its meat and leather and studied as a scientific mini-miracle. The emu, it seems, has laid its own golden egg.

The key to emu's indestructibility is that it can eat almost anything – dry leaves, twigs, even bark, though it is partial to young crops and greens if it can get them. To demonstrate, Fry holds out a lettuce leaf to one of his charges at Taronga Zoo. With a strange pig-like grunt, the large male grabs the leaf.

As it savours the delicacy, I examine its dense beige and black plumage. The feathers are coarse and stringy, and beneath the pelt I feel a heavily muscled thigh, powerful as an Olympic sprinter's. Each leg ends in three toes; the middle one, tipped with a wicked-looking black claw, is about 15 centimetres long. "They use that as their fighting weapon," Fry explains.

To see how these extraordinary birds behave in the wild, I join Terry Dawson, Professor of Zoology at the University of New South Wales, on an expedition near Broken Hill. At dawn Dawson, who has spent the past nine years studying emus, starts the engine of his four-wheel drive. "We should see a mob before long," he says. "More than a million roam the outback and they start foraging at first light." For long minutes we shudder and bounce over stunted bushes and sparse native grasses, with no sign of life. Then Dawson abruptly brakes and kills the engine. He points silently ahead at a line of dark shapes moving against the flame-red horizon.

We leave the vehicle and edge slowly forward. Soon I can see the emus clearly, striding through the saltbush, pecking at titbits without breaking stride. Suddenly the emus freeze. Their

*Although no mental giant, the emu nevertheless knows a few secrets that medical researchers would like to share – its body oil contains a powerful anti-inflammatory ingredient that may help people suffering with arthritis.*

leader, bigger than the rest, rears up, shaking his shaggy plumage, and begins to hiss. Then he puffs up his neck feathers and weaves his neck from side to side like a snake about to strike. I take a nervous step back. "It's just an aggression ritual," Dawson explains. "It won't last long."

As if on cue, the mob turns tail and accelerate away, necks horizontal, legs reaching out in long strides. Dawson points to footprints left on the ground. "They're about three metres apart," he calculates. "When the birds are in a real hurry, they can cover four metres in a single stride."

Temperatures of 40 degrees are normal out here, and just about everything about the emu's physiology is designed to cope with the heat. "Their noses contain special structures that can evaporate moisture to cool the blood flowing through them," Dawson explains. "This blood then circulates back through a highly complex network of vessels to cool the arterial blood flowing to the brain." But the emus' main protectors are the strange, stringy feathers I felt at Taronga Zoo.

On the plain near Broken Hill, one of Dawson's Ph.D. students has set up an experiment to test the pelt's insulating properties. "Meet Eric," says Shane Maloney, a powerfully built zoology graduate. Maloney's "bird" consists of a plank and a 20-litre plastic drum of water covered by what looks like a dirty shag-pile carpet.

"That's the pelt," says Maloney, who has been up since dawn monitoring his experiment. The crude-looking dummy is anything but primitive. Hidden between pelt and drum are sensors connected to a laptop computer measuring temperature and heat flow. A thermostat in the drum maintains the water at emu body temperature of 38 degrees.

Maloney has shown that the emu's pelt is an efficient insulator. The black feather tips absorb radiation at the outer edge of the plumage, which means heat is kept away from the emu's body. "It's the opposite of a polar bear's fur," Maloney explains, "which transmits the sun's heat to the body." His monitor shows the temperature on the surface of the black-tipped feathers is a sweltering 60 degrees; underneath the pelt it isn't going above 39 degrees.

Eric is not the most convincing simulation – yet in the dust surrounding him are dozens of three-toed footprints, evidence that real emus have been here to investigate. Could they have been fooled into thinking Eric was a real bird?

"Certainly," says Dawson.

Strangely, this genius of survival is no mental giant. That's a fact well known to Aborigines, who have hunted emus for food for thousands of years. "Traditional hunters used to hide in a bush and attract a bird's attention by rustling the branches and imitating its call," explains Malcolm Clark, an Aborigine from Broken Hill. "When an emu approached, the hunters

*The eggs are tended by the male bird, who protects and gently turns them until the pigeon-sized chicks are ready to peck their way out into the world.*

jumped out and whacked it over the head with a nulla nulla."

Oddest of all, this extraordinary bird's future looks even more remarkable than its past. In 1975-76 the Government set up a pilot emu farm at Wilura, almost 1000 kilometres from Perth on the fringe of the Gibson Desert. Now called Kalaya Emu Farm (*kalaya* is the Aboriginal word for emu), it was handed over to the Ngangganawilli community in 1981. Today Kalaya, with an annual turnover of almost half a million dollars, is just one of 50 or so commercial farms across Australia that raise around 40,000 birds each year to fill a growing demand for emu steak and leather.

I watch Kalaya manager Gary Ashwin at the edge of a paddock as he tops up a big metal drum with wheat. Milling around and jostling him are a mass of young adult emus. "They can guzzle up to one-and-a-half kilos of food a day," says Ashwin, a lanky ex-stockman.

An emu larger than the others approaches. Without warning, it pecks at my boot studs. Then, as I back away, it lunges at my camera, hooking its neck through the strap. Alarmed, I shout, "Hey!" and the animal takes fright, straining away from me. After a brief struggle the strap slides off the bird's neck, and the animal retreats to a safe distance. Grinning, Ashwin explains that emus go for anything bright, swallowing coins, keys, stones, glass, bits of tin can, spark plugs.

"Pickings are lean in the outback," he says, "so an emu will react to anything that stands out." To the bird's tiny brain, my boot studs might have looked like black acacia seeds, he says, and my camera lens, the shimmering wings of an insect.

Ashwin drives me to a free-range nesting paddock, a 12-hectare enclosure from which eggs are taken to be artificially incubated – guaranteeing a hatching rate twice as high as in the wild. Ashwin points to a rumpled mat of dead grass among

the scrub. "Here's a nest," he says, bending down and brushing aside the stalks to reveal three dark-green eggs, like giant avocados. "The bird that laid these may set down a few more, so we'll hold off collecting the clutch for now." He marks the site by ramming a post into the ground.

In the wild, the emu mother abandons her eggs and allows the father to take over all parental duties. In an epic feat of endurance, he goes without food or water for eight weeks, sustained only by his reserves of fat, until the eggs hatch. Then he cares for the hatchlings for up to 18 months, until they can fend for themselves. This reversal of sex roles helps to ensure the survival of the species – while the male tends the eggs, the female may mate with another male, producing a total of a dozen or so eggs in the winter breeding season.

Rounding a patch of mulga, we spy a plump emu, head and neck flat to the ground. Except for its glinting eyes, it appears dead. "He's alive all right," says Ashwin. "He's camouflaging himself." Ashwin circles behind the bird, grabs it under its wings and pushes. It makes a booming noise like a bass drum, then lopes away. Ashwin finds five eggs and transfers them to a plastic tray. The male quickly returns, poking his beak around

*Wild emus occupy a range of habitats in Australia, from the arid plains to alpine regions. They start to forage at daybreak and not even the midday sun can deter them.*

the plundered nest before wandering off dejectedly. "He'll perk up when he meets his mate again," says Ashwin.

In the incubator shed, kept at a constant 35 degrees Celsius, 2200 eggs are laid out on spindle-mounted trays. Replicating what the male emu does in the wild, the eggs are rolled gently every three hours to prevent the embryos sticking to the shells. "The eggs are unbelievably strong," says Max Sutton, the incubator manager. "You'd need to hit hard to crack one." He shows me a shard of shell. It's two millimetres thick.

Next we visit the hatcher unit, where the eggs are moved after seven weeks in the incubator. The hatchlings instinctively "pip" the eggs from within, making a triangular gouge with their beaks. Then they slowly enlarge the opening, sometimes taking several hours, before hatching. A dozen or so chicks, striped creamy-white and black, have hatched here in the past six hours. The size of pigeons, they huddle round infra-red bulbs for extra warmth. At three weeks, they'll be moved to an outdoor enclosure during the day. At around four months, they are trucked 740 kilometres to a "grow-out" farm at Three Springs to mature, until, at around 12 months, they are sent to one of the two processing plants in Australia.

Production of low-fat, high-protein emu meat (with a beef-like flavour) has increased dramatically. Several farmers have negotiated multi-million-dollar contracts with France. Very little of the bird is wasted in the processing: each carcass yields more than 0.6 square metres of fine, stippled leather, which is increasingly sought by the fashion industry; feathers are sold as stuffing for cushions and toys; the toe claws are mounted on pieces of jewellery; and the eggs are carved to reveal paler layers of green and sold as ornaments.

But farmers believe the income from these commodities is pocket money compared to the earning potential of emu oil.

Each adult bird has up to eight litres of the oil trapped in a thick layer of fat beneath its skin, acting as an energy and water reserve like a camel's hump.

Aborigines and early European settlers touted the oil as a skin balm and remedy for arthritis, but only recently has its reputation made the leap from folklore to fact. A team of medical researchers led by Sydney University's Professor Peter Ghosh, a bone and joint expert, and Dr Michael Whitehouse, a pharmacologist at the University of Adelaide, began a series of tests on emu oil. Laboratory rats were injected with dead bacteria to produce arthritis. Emu oil was then applied to a shaven patch on their backs.

The results were startling. After a few days the rats showed only minimal swelling and inflammation. "Emu oil contains a potent anti-inflammatory substance," Ghosh explains. The emu's money-earning potential has already spread to the United States, where the birds are so sought after that ranchers will pay between $40,000 and $60,000 for a breeding pair. Prices like this have even spawned a new crime – emu rustling. In Texas, millions of dollars worth of emus have been reported missing since 1991. In 1992 the FBI helped track down $300,000 worth of stolen emu chicks belonging to rancher Jody Giddens. They were identified thanks to microchips he had injected into the young birds' rumps.

It's all a far cry from the days when emus were shot on sight. Now, with farmers on their side, emus are entering a golden age. "What better bird to farm in Australia than the emu," says Gary Fry. "It belongs here."

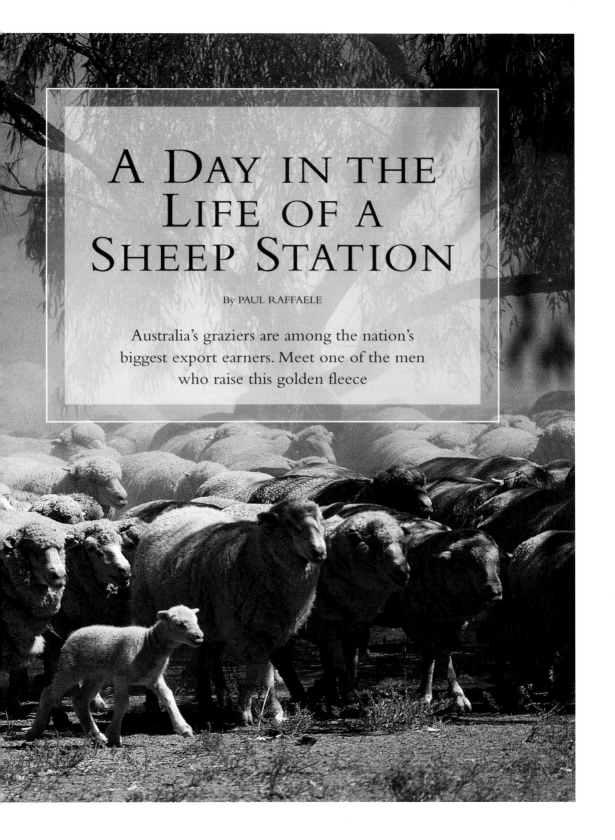

# A Day in the Life of a Sheep Station

By PAUL RAFFAELE

Australia's graziers are among the nation's
biggest export earners. Meet one of the men
who raise this golden fleece

6 a.m.: The harsh clang of an ancient alarm clock sounds in the master bedroom of Myandetta, a 20,000-hectare sheep station near Bourke in northwestern New South Wales. Grazier John Davis walks to the windows, and his eyes sweep the dawn sky, seeking any hint of cloud. There has been no decent summer rainfall for five years. His worst fear is a complete drought.

6:16 a.m.: John's wife, Merril, is away visiting their daughter, Narelle, in Orange, so John listens to the radio while he cooks himself breakfast. Wool prices remain steady, says the newsreader. Davis, still wiry and athletic at the age of 61, attacks his mutton chops and eggs with gusto. He can hear his two sheep dogs stirring impatiently outside the back door. "Can't keep the sheep waiting," he says as he puts on a sweat-stained Akubra and strides out of the house.

When John's grandfather, Ebenezer, started Myandetta in the early 1900s, he built the homestead close to a bend in the majestic Darling River. As John walks the dusty road to the woolshed a few hundred metres away, a dozen fat-gutted pelicans stretch their wings on the riverbank, readying themselves for a day of fishing. Across the river, several grey kangaroos settle in the shade to laze away the hot day. There will be no such idling for John: today, March 1, is another shearing day, the muscle-straining climax to another year of hard yakka.

Outside the woolshed John greets his son Michael, 30, who lives nearby with his wife, Barbara, and two children. Some 300 sheep have spent the night in the woolshed pens, ready for an early start. "There's room for another 500," John tells his son, who immediately kickstarts his 250-cc Suzuki motorbike. Practised motorcyclists, Michael's two kelpies jump on board, one on Michael's knees, the other perched on the rear. "Mustering a mob of sheep on a horse would take me half

*Previous page: A large flock of Merinos, mustered and ready for shearing, on Myandetta Station, near Bourke, New South Wales.*

a day or more," he says. "With the bike I can have them by the woolshed in an hour."

6:55 a.m.: The crackle of the Suzuki and a rolling cloud of dust announce the arrival of the new mob of sheep. As they near the pens, a dozen or so animals make a break for it, and John and Michael's dogs spin around and give chase. Nipping at the sheep's hooves, they force them back into the fast-moving flock.

7 a.m.: Entering the spacious woolshed, John Davis greets the five shearers, who are already oiling their high-speed electric shears. "Let's have the first of the day," says head shearer Peter Orcher. He grabs a 55-kilo wether, a castrated ram, by its forelegs and drags it across the floor. Orcher pulls its back against his knees and tucks its head into his stomach. Starting from its belly, he expertly peels off the heavy fleece. Two minutes later Orcher pushes the now-naked animal back through his legs, propelling it down a narrow, sloping chute to an outside pen. In the few seconds it takes the sheep to skitter down, Orcher has the next one ready for shearing.

A roustabout grabs the six-kilo fleece, thick with grease and stained with red dust, and flings it onto a table next to Michael Davis, a qualified wool classer. Michael quickly parts the wool, revealing thick, springy, snow-white fibre. His expert eye takes in its crimp, softness, colour,

*A young wether that has somehow become separated from the flock must be rescued and returned to its companions.*

*Graziers prize their dogs — a well-trained animal can muster a flock of sheep more efficiently than two men.*

length and weight. He plucks a strand from the fleece, snapping it against his fingers to test its pliancy. Satisfied, he drops the fleece into a large bin. Like most station owners around Bourke, John raises Merino sheep and produces medium-density "bread-and-butter" wool used to make an all-purpose cloth. Much of it is sold to Western Europe, Japan and Asia.

7:45 a.m.: Eight-year-old Kristy, Michael's daughter, roars round the homestead on her child-sized motorbike. Clinging to her waist is her four-year-old brother, Bradley. Like sheep-station children of another era who learned to ride a horse as soon as they could walk, most graziers' children can ride a motorbike at an early age. Kristy parks the bike and climbs into her mother's four-wheel-drive Subaru for the 40-kilometre drive to school in Bourke. Barbara makes the round trip twice each weekday, covering 800 kilometres a week. "Kristy is much luckier than kids in isolated stations, who have to learn by correspondence and the School of the Air," she says.

8:30 a.m.: "Hey...hey...hey!" John Davis shouts and flaps his arms as he and the dogs muster 100 more sheep for shearing. A young ewe, frightened by John's yells, charges back into the flock. The sheep bunch in panic, and there is a chance some of the lambs may be crushed to death. One dog sees the problem and leaps over the fence, landing on the backs of the closely packed sheep. Running halfway across the flock on top of the animals, the dog then ferrets his way down to the ground. Snapping at the churning hooves of the sheep, he turns part of the flock back, easing the pressure on those ahead.

Training a sheep dog is a lengthy business and starts within two months of its birth. "At eight weeks, a good puppy will be herding fowl in the backyard," John says with a grin. "Around that age, we'll take him down to the pens and let him watch the older dogs work the sheep." Graziers prize their dogs. "One dog is worth two men," John continues. Their four dogs enable father and son to run the huge station on their own for much of the year.

9:30 a.m.: It's "smoko" time – a 30-minute rest break for the shearers, who work four back-breaking two-hour stints. Orcher has already shorn 53 sheep, right on line for his target of 200 a day. At around $1.30 a sheep, it's a lucrative trade for hard-muscled men.

The holding pens behind the shearing stands are almost full of shorn sheep. John Davis and a roustabout begin to herd them through the dip, to douse for lice. Davis wipes away a trickle of sweat from his face; the temperature has just passed 35 degrees Celsius and will go higher.

10:30 a.m.: On her way back from Bourke, Barbara has collected 40 snapping blue yabbies from lines she had placed in a billabong by the river. Now she plops them into boiling water on the stove. Looking out the window, Barbara sees Bradley peering at something on the ground. The freshly watered grass has attracted a highly poisonous western brown snake. Slamming the door behind her, she rushes outside and grabs the child, just in time to see the snake slither away, disturbed by all the commotion.

Noon: Father and son stroll to Michael's homestead for a meal of sweet yabbie meat. Twenty minutes is all they allow themselves – every minute of daylight counts during shearing season. "Can't muster sheep in the dark," says Michael.

After lunch Michael heads back to the woolshed, while his father sets off in his four-wheel-drive on a tour of some of Myandetta's artesian bores used for watering the sheep. It's a task he has to perform every two or three days, covering the entire station. A fouled trough or a malfunctioning windmill could easily cause a thousand or more sheep to die of thirst within a week.

On the far horizon John Davis spies clouds, but not the thick, dark kind he needs to water the paddocks and so produce a healthy growth of scrub to feed the sheep through winter. Drought is an old foe of the Davis family. In a terrible dry spell in the early '40s, they were forced to lease Myandetta to a neighbour. For nearly a decade young John worked in the western woolsheds, shearing, crutching, mustering, saving every spare penny to buy the family land from his grandfather. He finally bought Myandetta in 1950 at $1.30 an acre. Soon after came one of the biggest booms in wool prices.

2:36 p.m.: John Davis's practised eyes spot three sickly young wethers huddled beneath a tree, unable to get through a wire fence to a familiar watering hole. He quickly collars each one in turn, thrusting them through the fence and watching happily as they bound towards the water. "Sheep are remarkable animals," he says. "They have to scrounge over rough

countryside to get feed. The ewes must protect their lambs against marauding eagles, foxes, crows, even feral pigs. City folk tend to think sheep are stupid, but put a man out into this paddock to live like a sheep and he'd be dead in a matter of days."

4 p.m.: As John Davis arrives back at the woolshed, a roustabout is pressing the fleece into bales. Myandetta produces about 200 bales of wool a year, each weighing 190 kilos. Each year the Bourke railhead dispatches about 60,000 bales of wool to markets in Sydney, Newcastle and Brisbane. Australia's wool clip is worth billions of dollars.

4:15 p.m.: Having picked up Kristy from school, Barbara stops by Honeyman's general store, which serves more than 60 sheep stations all over western New South Wales. Roger Honeyman, a third-generation Bourke storekeeper, is putting together an order for a station 180 kilometres to the north-

*The dogs are quick to sense where the trouble lies and adept at finding the shortest route – often across the backs of the tightly bunched flock.*

west. A young assistant shouts out the order: "Twelve large cans of beans, 16 cans of tomatoes, two dozen loaves of bread, six cans of mushrooms, eight cartons of margarine, six dozen eggs, six pumpkins, five kilos of bacon, a leg of ham." The supplies will be delivered next day by mail truck.

The Honeymans' generosity is legendary. During a bad drought in the '80s, Roger supplied provisions on credit to more than a dozen cashless graziers for up to three years. "The banks wouldn't lend them any more money, so what else could I do?" he asks. "I knew they'd come good when wool prices picked up. Not one reneged."

"Out here families all know each other," says Barbara. "We've built up trust over the decades. There's a deep level of friendship in the outback you rarely find in the cities."

5 p.m.: It's knock-off time for the shearers. The outside pens hold more than 800 shorn and dipped sheep. "A good day's work," says Michael Davis, as he shoos the sheep from the pens. On a motorbike, his father drives them towards paddocks two kilometres away. There he will collect another mob for shearing first thing tomorrow.

6:30 p.m.: John Davis parks his bike in the woolshed and ambles home. On less busy days he might drive into Bourke for a few beers, but tonight a shower, a good meal and bed is what he wants most. First he must water and feed his dogs, one of the day's most important tasks.

The phone rings. It is a friend, Gordon Alderman, calling from the 16-hectare wool-selling complex at Yennora, near Sydney. "Hold off buying any more sheep for a while – the price is too high," he says. "But don't worry, with this year's clip you'll do all right."

7 p.m.: John sits down to a dinner of cold meat and potatoes. Normally, Merril would have prepared a hearty meal of

roast mutton and vegetables, but in her absence he has to make do. Even with wool cheques generous once again, Davis has no plans to extend his small homestead. The profits he ploughs back into Myandetta will build it up for Michael, who will in turn secure the station for Bradley. In the outback, the family still counts for far more than the individual.

8:55 p.m.: It's almost bedtime, and Davis is in a philosophical mood. "Sometimes, when there's been a drought and the sheep are dying off in front of my eyes," he says, "I come home all choked up. I say to Merril, 'Why bother going on? Let's just walk away, give up Myandetta.' But the next morning at sunrise, I look around, see the sheep in the paddocks, the parrots swarming about, and the sun on the river. I don't know any other way of living."

9:10 p.m.: Davis turns in. As the air conditioner drones on softly, he closes his eyes and instantly falls asleep. Tonight there is no need for him to count sheep.

*A routine check on the condition of the fleece. The Merino sheep raised on Myandetta station produce medium-density wool.*

*EDITORS' NOTE:*
*Soon after this article was written, John Davis's wife, Merril, died suddenly.*

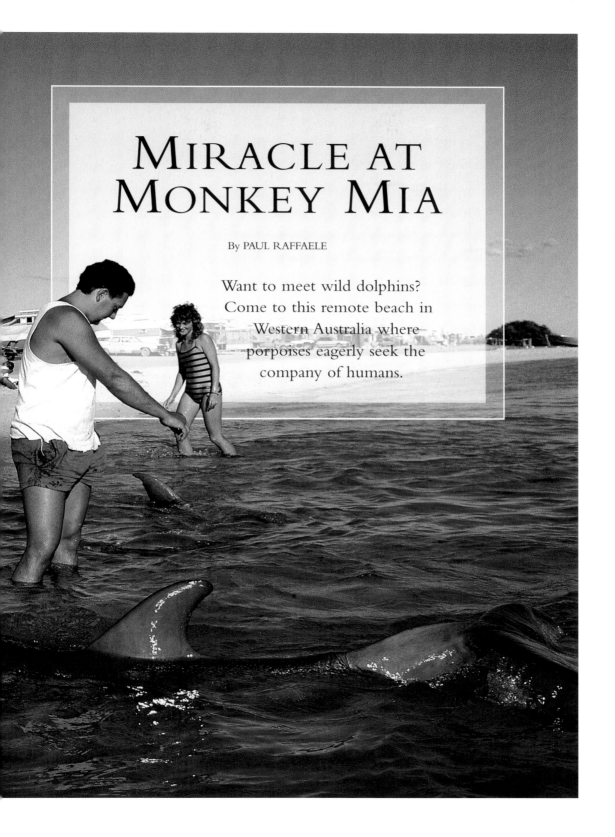

# MIRACLE AT MONKEY MIA

By PAUL RAFFAELE

Want to meet wild dolphins?
Come to this remote beach in
Western Australia where
porpoises eagerly seek the
company of humans.

D awn breaks over Monkey Mia, a small beach on Australia's extreme western shore. Low waves foam over my bare legs as I stand watching the brightening horizon. A dozen other people are keeping vigil with me, drawn here from all over the world by strange tales of wild dolphins who, we have heard, choose this place to frolic with humans in the shallows. There is a Japanese artist on her first trip abroad, a retired couple from England, four young friends from Brisbane, a Chicago businessman and a chiropractor from Stockholm.

Suddenly someone shouts, "There! Over there." About 100 metres out at sea, five dorsal fins simultaneously break the surface, then the dark shapes elegantly arch over sideways, revealing long, beaked faces. The wild dolphins!

Within seconds, speeding like torpedoes, they shoot right up to the water's edge. Fearlessly the swim past each of us in turn, rolling sideways to see us better with their dark eyes. I reach out a tentative hand towards a large male. He pauses as I touch his strongly muscled flank and responds by gently nudging me backwards. Then he rolls onto his back, exposing his pale belly, inviting me to scratch. I oblige, and he replies with a staccato burst of whistles and squeaks.

I am enthralled. So is the quiet artist from Japan, who squeals with delight as a dolphin nuzzles her hand. The elderly woman from England, knee-deep in the warm water, runs a hand along a young dolphin's back, her eyes shining with excitement. "How wonderful!" she cries. The rest, too, are spellbound, hardly believing what they see.

For a little longer dolphins whirl among us, then with a swish of their tails, they are off to deeper waters. I return to the beach to sit quietly on the sand, strangely moved. The others, too, are silent, stunned by the intensity of the experience.

*Previous page: Visitors come from all over the world to enjoy a unique experience: being greeted by wild dolphins in their own environment and on their own terms.*

Elsewhere in the world there have been isolated cases of single wild dolphins venturing into shallow water and briefly befriending people. But at Monkey Mia a small group comes in every day. "There's nowhere else like this," says Rachel Smolker, a University of Michigan zoologist who has been coming to Monkey Mia for years to research dolphin behaviour. "It's the best place to observe dolphins close up in the wild."

Locals credit Alice Watts, a trawler owner, with discovering the dolphins. One night in 1964 she was anchored off Monkey Mia with her husband in their boat *Maybe*. It was sweltering and Alice lay awake listening to the splashing of a dolphin that kept swimming round the boat. Finally she got up and took a yellowtail, which had been caught for bait, from the refrigerator and threw it into the water. The dolphin swam straight to the side of the boat and took it, she says. A week or so later he came back again, bringing his mate and baby. Eventually all three took fish from her hand.

*In these magical encounters, there is an absence of fear on both sides.*

Alice, known as Nin, named the dolphin Charlie and he became a mascot to the Monkey Mia fishing fleet. Nin insists that it was not food that attracted Charlie. "There is more than enough food in the bay, and dolphins are expert hunters," she says. Often he would toss fish back into the boat as if to demonstrate that it was only a game.

When Nin and her husband Ern went back to their base in Mandurah, 50 kilometres south of Perth, local fishermen adopted Charlie. Jim Poland, a beach seine fisherman, was among the first actually to touch the dolphin. "He brushed against the side of our small boat," says Poland. "On impulse,

*Although they are sometimes fed fish by tourists, under the supervision of rangers, food doesn't seem to be what attracts the dolphins to this very special place.*

*Facing page: Looking down on the gathering from the air, you realise how close inshore the dolphins are prepared to venture, surely a demonstration of trust that must not be betrayed.*

we reached out and pulled him on board, resting him on our knees. He seemed to enjoy the experience." Charlie began to wait for Poland's boat, meeting him two kilometres offshore and escorting him home to Monkey Mia. "He used to do flips and jumps above the water to entertain us."

Sadly, it was Charlie's friendliness that was his undoing. Poland found him dead on the beach one day, shot through the head, probably by rifle-happy kids.

But Charlie's family continued to frolic with the fishermen and gradually brought in other dolphins. Over the next few years, word of the dolphins gradually began to filter out. Groups of intrepid people now began to reach the beach via a rough pot-holed 24-kilometre track that wound its way through blood-red sand dunes from Denham, a small fishing village 850 kilometres north of Perth.

Among them were Wilf and Hazel Mason, who were so enchanted by the dolphins that they decided to stay and set up a caravan park. Wilf, a kindly man with sea-blue eyes, named

*Farther out in the bay, the gentle creatures swim with divers, an experience that has a profound effect on many.*

many of the dolphins. "People come here for only a short time," he says, "and want to identify the dolphins so they can understand them better. I gave them names to suit their character or looks."

Later that day, standing knee-deep in the azure water, I watched three generations of female dolphins at play in the shallows. The grandmother named Holey Fin careened up and down the beach, pausing to nuzzle anyone who took her fancy. Her granddaughter, Nipper, remained near to her mother, Nicky, who stayed five or six metres from shore.

As I watched Nipper's antics, the male, Snubnose, swam up and gently nudged my leg. Arching his body to lift his head completely out of the water, he offered me a single strand of brown seaweed that he had collected somewhere offshore. I took it, carefully examined it and then politely handed it back. This was obviously a favourite game. Clenching the strand between his teeth he swam off to offer it to another visitor.

Despite the temptation, Wilf has been careful not to teach the dolphins any tricks, recognising that it would rob them of their unique attraction and scientific value as wild animals. I was glad of his concern when I saw Sickle Fin and Snubnose leap out of the water in perfect unison some 40 metres offshore. For a fleeting moment they hovered together in the air before dropping back into the bay. No trainer had coached them in the routine – it was instinctive.

Rachel Smolker has often been astonished at the sophistication of dolphin behaviour. "We have learned that they have a society more complex than even higher primates such as chimpanzees and gorillas." she remarks.

Each day, weather permitting, Smolker goes out in a boat to observe the dolphins and record their vocalisations with an underwater microphone. For echo location, dolphins emit a variety of sounds from a large bulbous structure at the base of their foreheads. Within it are specialised fats that focus the sounds in front of the dolphin's head. A dolphin may be able to produce a burst of sound so intense that it can stun a fish.

Rachel's tapes of dolphin "conversations" sound like a farmyard in uproar. Ducks honk, pigs grunt and oink, dogs bark, cows moo, gates slam and electric saws buzz. Smolker once taped Snubnose having what she believed was a temper tantrum, jealous that a visitor to Monkey Mia was giving more fish to another dolphin. The sound is like an enraged elephant trumpeting. "I've even witnessed dolphins in heated argument, head to head in the water, yelling in dolphin language at each other," she says.

Smolker observed that eight dolphins came to the beach regularly. "They seem to be a core group of about 60, and we can study their actions in detail." Even those dolphins that don't come to the beach are not frightened of people. "They allow us to approach them in the boats, even when we are ten kilometres out in the bay."

Paul Anderson, Emeritus Professor of Biology at the University of Calgary in Canada, has studied the area's dugongs, large whale-like tropical mammals. Like others, he wonders why the Monkey Mia miracle has not been duplicated elsewhere and offers this explanation of why other local dolphins and dugongs are unafraid of man: "They have been able to roam the bay freely for thousands of years because the Aboriginal inhabitants did not have boats."

Sharon Gosper is one of six rangers who monitor the beach from dawn each morning to ensure that the dolphins are not annoyed or hurt. They were appointed after the local shire council became worried by the influx of visitors. I noticed, though, that when people became too boisterous, the dolphins seemed well able to look after themselves. Sickle Fin in particular was quick to bump, push or splash an errant tourist. One woman who persisted in tugging his fin was punished by two sharp bites on the finger. Other unruly visitors were given hard, painful thumps with his tail.

But the tidal wave of visitors, 200,000 or more in some seasons, concerns Smolker. Crooked Fin, a former regular has already opted out. "She still comes over to my boat" says Smolker, "but no longer mixes with people on the beach. It would be tragic if overcrowding were to end this unique communication between dolphins and humans."

There is dismay, too, among some locals in nearby Denham. "Our way of life is under threat," says Dick Hoult, president of the local fishermen's association. "Many townspeople are unhappy at the numbers coming to Monkey Mia."

Hoult discounts the possibility that some locals might be tempted to give tangible expression to their dislike: "None of us would ever harm a dolphin. We were brought up to believe that they bring good luck."

*Researchers think that the dolphins have lost all fear of humans because they have never been hunted. Aboriginal people in the area did not use boats.*

I thought of Hoult's words as I sat on the beach at dawn on my last day at Monkey Mia, waiting for a final encounter with the dolphins. Half an hour passed, then an hour. There was still no sign of them. Across the beach came an impatient honk from the early bus to Denham.

I picked up my bags. But as I walked to the waiting bus, a cry rang out: "They're back!" A single dolphin leapt three or four metres out of the water. To the right, six fins broke the surface and swept towards the beach.

The bus driver sounded his horn again and again, summoning those of us booked for the morning run. With childish glee and ignoring the insistent blare, I walked fully clad into the water. Holey Fin swam up to me and I reached down to stroke her gently along her side as she whistled and beeped. I watched as the bus departed and Monkey Mia's wondrous miracle unfolded once more.

# BEAUTIFUL,
# BOUNTIFUL
# BAROSSA

By JIM HUTCHISON and MARGO PFEIFF

Travel into the warm heart of
South Australia's great wine valley

"Hands off!" hot-air balloon pilot Simon Fisher calls to his launch crew, and our ten-storey-high nylon teardrop rises into a crisp autumn sky. Although the Barossa is just waking at this early hour, the grape pickers are already at work among rows of russet vines; they pause to wave to our craft.

As we ride a northward breeze up the valley, a scene from an old German watercolour unfolds — quaint towns dot the harvest patchwork of the valley floor, each with a stately Lutheran church spire winking silver in the sun. We glide over the steep-pitched roofs of stone cottages in tiny Bethany, with its thatched barns and village common. Beyond, scattered like jewels among farms, orchards and market gardens, stand grand winery châteaux with names that, as we learn later, include Kaiser Stuhl and Château Yaldara Estate.

From high in our wicker gondola, this could be classic European wine country. But as we prepare to descend into a pasture near Angaston, we skim the tops of river red gums, flushing out a cloud of rosellas and sending a trio of kangaroos hopping down a dusty side road — unmistakable clues as to the continent on which we are about to make a bumpy landing.

Within an hour's drive of Adelaide, the Barossa has long been a weekend retreat for city dwellers, who indulge in continental cuisine in the character-rich small towns and tastings in the old-world atmosphere of its wineries. Although the valley is only 32 kilometres long, it bottles a third of the country's vintage. Harvest time buzzes with activity, especially during the week-long Barossa Valley Vintage Festival that begins on Easter Monday every odd-numbered year. What began as a simple gathering of family and friends in 1947 is now the biggest wine festival in the southern hemisphere, attended by about 100,000 visitors.

*Previous page: From a vantage point in a hot-air balloon floating above the Barossa Valley, the vineyards at Seppeltsfield Estate could be somewhere in Europe. Only the river red gums give the clue as to where we are.*

Arriving at the valley's southern gateway of Lyndoch on the Easter Saturday before the festival, we go on the balloon trip to get an overview of the valley before setting off to explore the Barossa at a leisurely bicycle pace. The winding roads that thread together the four main valley towns – Lyndoch, Tanunda, Nurioopta and Angaston – are lined with vineyards and towering gum trees.

The pale summer-brown hills are ever present in the distance. South Australia's first surveyor-general, Colonel William Light, named the valley Lynedoch Vale in 1837 after Lord Lynedoch – "a much esteemed friend". Light called the ranges Barrosa (Hill of Roses) to commemorate the site of Lynedoch's Peninsula War victory. However, a draughtsman's error rendered them Barossa and Lyndoch on the first maps and the misspellings have stuck.

Family businesses have always been the backbone of the Barossa and in tiny wineries, such as The Willows, Bethany Wines and the Barossa Settlers Winery, a warm homespun character still shines through. Over a glass of riesling in the Barossa Settlers tasting room at Lyndoch, part-owner Joan Haese traces her family back four generations on this property. "We have always been grape growers, but establishing our own winery in 1983 fulfilled a life-long dream," she says.

We cross over Jacob's Creek, on whose banks in 1847 a Bavarian farmer named Johann Gramp planted the first vine cuttings that set the Barossa on its destined path. Almost a decade earlier, German geologist Johann Menge had reported: "I am certain that we shall see the place flourish, and vineyards

*Colourful German folk costumes are greatly in evidence during the week-long Barossa Valley Vintage Festival. Some 100,000 visitors flock to join in the convivial harvest celebrations.*

*The Tabor church in Tanunda, one of the town's seven churches ministering to a population of just 3200 souls.*

and orchards and immense fields of corn throughout. It will furnish huge quantities of wine. . ."

We pedal down the sleepy main street of Bethany, the valley's first settlement, laid out in medieval style with its stone cottages fronting the road and narrow strips of pasture out behind. In the cemetery we find the names of the Barossa's original settlers engraved in Gothic German script on the weathered marble headstones. These were devout Silesian Lutherans who endured religious persecution under Prussia's Friedrich Wilhelm III. Rather than allow the king to dictate their faith, they prepared to flee their homeland. When wealthy businessman George Fife Angas, owner of more than 11,000 hectares in the Barossa, heard of the planned exodus, he financed their escape, convinced they would make fine colonists.

Led by Pastor August Kavel, the first 200 Lutherans disembarked at Port Adelaide in 1838. Four years later, 28 families had settled in the Barossa and built this hamlet they named after the biblical Bethany. Many of these settlers became farmers to supply the colony with food. Others pursued trades as cobblers, carpenters or bakers. Poignant reminders of their hardships linger. Near Springton stands the old hollow red gum where Friedrich Herbig and his wife, Caroline, began married life and raised two of their 16 children.

By mid-afternoon we cycle into busy Tanunda, which, like all Barossa towns, is dedicated to the art of good eating. The counter at the Tanunda Wurst Haus is piled with home-made goods, from jars of pickled onions and gherkins to a bewildering assortment of cheeses and German sausages. Country bakeries, such as the cottage of Linke's at Nurioopta, are stuffed with *streuselkuchen*, *bienenstich*, *apfelstrudel* and freshly baked German breads. Above the sawdusted wooden floors of Schulz's butcher shop in Angaston, salami and *bierwurst* dangle like plump stalactites from bars attached to the ceiling.

In the evening, we dine on *sauerbraten* and *kasslerrippchen* in Tanunda. To our horror, in the middle of an oom–pah–pah recital by the town band, Neville Alderslade, a band member, raises the business end of a Lee Enfield .303 rifle to his lips. But instead of public suicide, he blows into a trumpet mouthpiece he has fitted to the rifle and treats us to a rousing rendition of the Post Horn Galop.

Since the first settlers arrived, music and song have been a way of life. The Tanunda Liedertafel – "songs round the table" – Choir has been a traditional Barossa men's singing society since 1861. The St Petri's Ladies Singalong Group regularly makes the rounds of rest homes, bringing cheer to the valley's elderly. "In the Barossa, people help one another," says Pastor Dennis Obst of the St Petri Lutheran Church at Nurioopta.

*A château that would look quite at home in the glorious Loire Valley, in France, houses Yaldara Estate's collection of porcelain and antique furniture.*

"With about half of the valley's residents being of German descent, there's a family atmosphere whether or not people are related."

The next morning, Easter Sunday, church bells peal throughout the length of the valley. For a population of only 18,000, most of

them Lutherans, of course, the Barossa has 36 churches. Tanunda alone, a town of 3200, has seven churches. "Some church bells in the valley are more than a century old and were brought from Germany," says John Stiller, music director of St Petri Church.

With the grape harvest in full swing, a steady stream of trucks passes us on the road between Tanunda and Nurioopta. They are loaded with the red and white grapes that thrive in the rich red-brown earth and alluvial soils of the Barossa. Twin rows of splendid date palms line the two-kilometre avenue to Marananga and the grand Australian colonial-style winery of Seppeltsfield.

Founded in 1851 by Joseph Seppelt, Seppeltsfield is today a complex of graceful bluestone buildings set on four hectares. Reinhold Koehler, cellar master for 34 years, takes us through Cellar Number One, musty and sweet smelling from row upon row of huge oak casks that ooze sticky residue from maturing port put aside every year since 1878. Seppelt's Para Liqueur, the most expensive Australian wine, is released when it's 100 years old. An 1885 bottle released in 1985 sold for $2000, or $100 for a 50-millilitre taste. Koehler points out barrels labelled "Prince Charles", "Prince Harry" and "Prince William", each laid down as a royal gift the year they were born. "On a visit to Australia," Koehler reveals, "Prince Charles requested that several bottles be drawn from his keg to be taken with him."

But the king of Barossa success stories is wine maker Wolfgang Blass, who came to Australia from Germany as a winery consultant in 1961. In the 33 years since he put down his first vintage, in a tin shed just outside Nurioopta, he has built a

*At many vineyards, grapes are still picked by hand, while at others, mechanical harvesting has taken over the back-breaking job.*

multi-million-dollar industry, selling hundreds of thousands of cases of wine every year. Wolf Blass wines have won more than 2000 national and international awards.

On the last stretch of our cycling trip – from Nurioopta to Angaston – we discover it is not only Germans who came to make wine in the valley. Near Angaston are William Salter's Saltram Winery and Samuel Smith's Yalumba, both founded by British pioneers. Yalumba is the oldest family-owned winery in the valley.

The wineries of the Barossa are a delight to the eye. A château that would look at home in France's Loire River Valley houses Château Yaldara's museum of 18th-century furniture and porcelain; Karlsburg is a turreted replica of a castle. But within their walls hums some of the world's most advanced

*In the tiny town of Tanunda, the population figures take a sharp leap during the biennial wine festival.*

wine-making machinery. While teams of chemists work in wine laboratories, computers aid their control systems.

"Despite the invasion of the cellar by computers," says Andres Markides, head of the Division of Wine Science at Roseworthy Agricultural College, which has been teaching viticulture in the valley since the turn of the century, "the age-old art of creating outstanding wines still lies with the experience and judgment of the master wine maker."

"We regularly receive wine delegations from Europe and the United States," says Rob Edwards of Tarac Industries. "The French especially are impressed with the diversity and quality of our wines and their low prices. There, champagne is made in the Champagne region, burgundy in Burgundy, but a single Barossa winery will often make red and white wines, ports, sherries and champagne."

*Huge casks of maturing wines line the walls of the Seppeltsfield winery, which also produces Seppelt's Para Liqueur, Australia's most expensive port. This prized vintage port is not released until it has matured for 100 years.*

Australia's romance with the grape is a comparatively recent affair. In the 1950s when we were a nation of beer and sherry drinkers, Max Schubert of Penfolds, now the biggest winery in the valley, appropriated refrigeration equipment meant to produce fortified wine. He needed the equipment to control fermentation in his quest to make "a decent red". His efforts first appeared in 1952 as Grange Hermitage, now one of the country's most famous wines. Australia's annual consumption of wine has doubled since the end of the 1960s to around 20 litres per person. But it is still well behind the French and Italian annual consumption of 90 litres per person.

We awake on Easter Monday in a two-room stone bungalow left over from a turn-of-the-century Barossa gold rush that saw 4000 prospectors pan 100,000 ounces before the lode petered out. The Miner's Cottage, now restored as an old-fashioned inn, overlooks a billabong where rainbow-coloured lorikeets decorate the gum trees like ornaments. The peaceful setting is in sharp contrast to the noise and revelry found in the towns.

Throughout the week of the wine festival, Barossa towns throw parties of feasting, *weingartens*, craft shows, music and dancing. Coopers demonstrate their keg-making skills and all eyes are on the feet during energetic grape-treading competitions. Growers, vintners and pickers test old-fashioned grape-picking skills, their hands a blur of movement as they race to fill buckets, while huge, modern harvesters lumber down the rows, plucking grapes by the tonne like mechanical locusts.

The Tanunda town square is packed as local folk sell produce and auction livestock. At Bilyara Vineyard, a rare-wine auction brings bids from New York, London and around Australia by Telecom satellite linkup as 1200 serious wine buffs gather for a champagne breakfast. About $150,000 is spent and, as with many Vintage Festival activities, some of the proceeds go to charity.

We and 1300 other revellers at the traditional Friday night Weingarten Dinner in the cavernous Tanunda Show Hall enjoy the best of Barossa hospitality and cheer in four courses of German cuisine and vintage wines. Saturday's procession of colourful floats travels from Nurioopta to Tanunda, culminating in a fair and concert. The festival's Sunday finale is a gala of parades and concerts at Angaston, named after George Fife Angas, who would surely be heartened to see what his fine colonists have wrought in their first 160-odd years. Johann Menge, too, could take a bow: the Barossa has indeed become one of the world's great wine valleys.

*A craftsman demonstrates the traditional technique of making stave barrels by hand. Despite increasing use of stainless steel, wooden barrels are still preferred for producing quality wines.*

# RIDING WITH THE HELICOPTER COWBOYS

By PAUL RAFFAELE

Join these outback daredevils for an
exhilarating high-tech round-up

I t is an unusually warm day for June, 34 degrees Celsius, as a mob of cattle heads across the parched earth of Victoria River Downs (VRD), a Northern Territory cattle station a quarter the size of Denmark. Mustering the cattle is a group of horse-riding stockmen who whoop and curse to keep the 1800 Poll Shorthorn-Brahmans moving towards a nearby holding pen.

As the red dust of the outback swirls about the animals, it seems as if nothing has changed since the Top End was tamed by graziers more than a century ago. But only metres above the bellowing herd hovers a helicopter. The steady *chop, chop, chop* of its rotor blades drives the animals forward, while the stockmen keep them in line. Pilot Geoff Selvey darts his machine back and forth across the plain, flushing cattle from clumps of bush and careering along dry creek-beds, swooping between the gum tree trunks to drive strays towards the herd.

This heart-stopping flying is a six-day-a-week routine for Selvey and some 80 other helicopter pilots who work in Australia's outback each year from March until the end of November. Their daredevil skills are the backbone of the country's multi-million-dollar export meat industry.

Until the early 1970s, it took weeks, sometimes months, for stockmen riding highly trained horses to herd large mobs of cattle to holding yards on the way to market. Now choppers do most of the work. "Skilled mustering by chopper is faster, cleaner and more efficient," says Mike Back, executive director of the Northern Territory Cattlemen's Association. "In one day, a single pilot can muster the same number of cattle as eight stockmen can in three or four weeks."

The immense Victoria River Downs, 250 kilometres southwest of Katherine, is serviced by Heli-Muster, the biggest of the Top End's helicopter mustering companies. I join half-a-

*Previous page: Heart-stopping flying is just routine to the 80 or so outback helicopter pilots who are the backbone of the country's export meat industry.*

dozen pilots clad in jeans, T-shirts and cowboy boots as they emerge from their caravans and bungalows at dawn. Chief pilot Selvey waves goodbye to his wife, Joanne, and their three-year-old daughter, Jessica, and leads the men towards eight small helicopters lined up on a splash of green grass in front of a hangar.

"Best time of day," says Selvey, sniffing the fresh, moist air. Fellow pilot Andy Page nods agreement. Like many of Heli-Muster's best pilots, Page was born in the bush. For seven years he herded cattle on horseback. Seeing chopper pilots at work, he patiently saved $18,000 to pay for the 70 hours of flight training needed for a commercial licence. "Much the same rules that apply in the saddle apply in a chopper," Page says. "You might be the best pilot in Australia, but if you don't know how cattle think, you won't be successful out here."

*Helicopter pilots are able to dart back and forth across the plain, flushing out stray cattle and forcing them on to join the herd.*

*Helicopter pilot Geoff Selvey plans the muster with station manager Ian Rush. Sky cowboys must know cattle as well as being able to fly.*

John Keir, also born in the outback, agrees. "Cattle live out in the scrub and don't have any human contact from year to year," he adds. "You've got to be cunning as a dunny rat to get them to do what you want."

Keir is carrying a swag, a sleeping bag rolled up in a tarpaulin. He's flying out to a mustering job at Mallapunyah, 490 kilometres distant, and will be away for a week or more, bedding down beside his helicopter. Sleeping rough is routine for these men: the company has 28 helicopters, but there are rarely more than eight or nine at its base. The others are spread across the Top End, from the Roper River in the east to the Kimberleys in the west.

As we talk, hundreds of sulphur-crested cockatoos and pink and grey galahs in the trees around the hangar break into a raucous dawn chorus. Then, rising as one, they screech across the base towards the nearby Victoria River. "Time to fly!" Selvey says with a grin as he climbs into his chopper. Much as a cowboy would pat the neck of his horse, Selvey pumps the floor pedals to get the feel of his mechanical steed, then switches on the motor. As the overhead rotor blades begin to spin, he dons his helmet – a triumphant gold affair adorned with a fighting kangaroo wearing red boxing gloves, aviator's goggles and a white scarf.

When the blades reach top speed, around 320 rpm, Selvey pulls back on the powerstick and we shoot up into the sky. Both doors have been removed from the chopper, and an icy wind slices through the tiny cabin as we head for Moolooloo, a VRD outstation about 55 kilometres to the east. Later in the day the wind will provide us with natural air-conditioning. Selvey steers the chopper above the settlement, passing over VRD's homestead, post office, general store, clinic, tennis court and a score of tin-roofed houses. Snaking around Moolooloo is the broad, muddy Victoria River, and Selvey drops down to skim along a few metres above the surface. Lazing crocodiles dive in fright as we zoom along the twisting waterway.

Our destination is a 300-square-kilometre paddock where we will drive 1800 head of cattle into a holding pen to be tested for tuberculosis. Infected stock will be slaughtered. For the TB clearance to work, not a single animal must remain in the paddock. Inevitably, a few wily old bulls and cows will elude us, says Selvey. Four or five days later a pilot will fly back to the paddock with a stock inspector who will gun down any cattle found inside its boundaries. Only then can stock that tested disease-free be released back into their home paddock.

Below us now is Moolooloo. Trees are thin on the arid, rocky ground, mostly tall eucalypts strung along the fringes of Battle Creek, the largely dry watercourse that cuts across

*Geoff Selvey refuels from a barrel trucked in for the purpose. The fuel must be pumped into the chopper's tank by hand.*

Moolooloo like a tribal initiation scar. As we pass over Moolooloo's barbed-wire boundary, the cattle scatter. "They know we're after them, and they're heading for cover," Selvey shouts over the roaring engine. He points across the sky to another chopper. "Andy over there will be mustering with us."

Page and Selvey begin flying a coordinated grid pattern, up and down the paddock, swooping low over small mobs of cattle, using the noise of the chopper to urge them into Battle Creek. Often, to see a hiding bull more clearly, Selvey cuts speed to zero and turns the chopper virtually on its side. Only the pilot's skill and our seatbelts save us from plunging through the open doors.

Once the cattle are in the dry watercourse, Page pushes them forward at a slow, steady pace, hovering behind the mob at a height of 100 metres. Their destination is a holding paddock 15 kilometres up the track, about as far as choppers muster cattle in a single day. The animals trudge along in twos and threes, heads bent, the long column trailed by a cloud of red dust. "The secret is not to put stress on the cattle," explains Selvey. "Just keep them calm. It's usually the cleanskins, the ones that have never been caught and so have not been branded, that give us trouble."

As Selvey flies, his practised eyes pick out cattle below where I can see only rocks, shrubs and trees. "Gotcha!" Selvey calls as he spots a bull lurking in a clump of bushes. He sets off in pursuit. Ranged around him in the cockpit are four controls, all of which must often be manipulated at the same time. The collector lever alters the pitch of the rotor blades, adjusting the lifting force. Attached to the collector is the throttle, which regulates the engine rpm. The cyclic lever tilts the whole rotor, like a giant gyroscope, moving the helicopter forwards, backwards or sideways. Two foot pedals control the small tail rotor, which acts like a rudder, keeping the helicopter in a straight line or turning it.

As we near the bull, Selvey thrusts the cyclic forward with his right hand, tilting the chopper at a steep angle, his feet manipulating the pedals, his left hand gripping the throttle while he pushes down on the collector to sink the helicopter towards the ground. Then he dives among the trees of the creek, rotor blades slicing the air only metres from the boughs.

After hurtling down the watercourse, Selvey pulls back the cyclic, stopping the helicopter two or three metres directly above the fleeing bull. The animal snorts in anger, turns and faces the chopper, eager to trample it into the ground. Selvey smiles at the brave challenge. As the blades chop furiously at the air over the bull's head, it charges a few steps, hesitates, suddenly loses courage and surrenders. Meekly, it joins the mob. Selvey pulls back the powerstick and we soar back into the sky.

It is a performance of breathtaking skill, but Selvey continues as if nothing has happened. "No, I never get shaky-legged in a chopper," he replies to my question. "Too much to think about."

Despite Selvey's brave words, this is a high-risk profession. In 1989, pilot John Armstrong was herding cattle into a VRD holding yard – one of the most dangerous tasks in mustering, with up to four choppers working at close range and dust blown up by the rotors' downblast often obscuring pilots' vision. A bull broke loose and Armstrong whirled the chopper around just metres off the ground, but pulled to the left a little too sharply. The machine lost speed and dropped so low that a rotor blade hit the ground. The chopper cartwheeled and crashed through a fence. Fortunately, Armstrong and his co-pilot walked away without a scratch.

Fate is not always so kind. "Choppers carry about 200 litres of fuel in containers right by the engine," says Heli-Muster engineer John Cunningham. "Pilots can survive a crash, but be burnt to death when the fuel explodes." To help ensure the pilots' survival, engineers routinely check the choppers after 100 hours of flying time. After 1200 to 2000 hours, depending on model, engineers strip down and reassemble the engine and transmission, or pull the entire helicopter apart and rebuild it.

Back over Moolooloo, the sun burns cruelly through the plastic bubble of Selvey's cockpit. We've been flying for two hours and fuel is getting low. Selvey puts the chopper down on a narrow track where a stash of fuel barrels has been trucked in. With the blades whirling just a few centimetres above his head, he pulls out a length of black hose, attaches it to a barrel, hand-pumps the fuel into his tank and takes off again.

After two more refuelling stops, Selvey and Page have herded virtually all 1800 cattle along Battle Creek, through a funnel made of barbed wire and hessian cloth into the holding paddock. To prevent them from milling around the fence, trying to return home, the pilots urge the cattle forward across a small hill to a couple of subartesian bore ponds, where the stock eagerly gulp cool water.

"Think I'll take a last look," Selvey radios to Page as he swings his machine's tail round a full 180 degrees. A low-flying inspection of the whole paddock convinces him it is clean. Heading back towards the holding pen, he swoops low over seven huge wedge-tailed eagles feeding on the carcass of a bustard. Frightened by the chopper's roar, they take to the sky, and Selvey plays follow-the-leader with one of the birds, imitating its graceful movements in an aerial *pas de deux*.

Breaking off, he points to the trees below, where a large black-and-white stork is making its stately progress along Battle Creek. "It's things like this," he says, "that make me realise how lucky I am to have this job."

At 4 p.m., the two men head for home. The cockatoos and galahs are back in their roosts when Selvey lands at the base 20 minutes later. After a shower, he joins the other pilots for a quick drink before going home for dinner. "You don't survive long in this game if you are a heavy drinker," Selvey says. "A hangover could prove fatal." As he approaches his bungalow, his small daughter, Jessica, runs to greet him, and he bends down to scoop her up.

Despite the daily danger, Selvey says he can't imagine a life that would give him greater satisfaction. "In five years I've racked up almost 5000 chopper hours mustering cattle," he says with a smile, "and I reckon I'll be in the saddle for a few more years yet."

*Andy Page completes the day's mustering by herding the cattle into the yard. This is one of the most dangerous jobs in the muster, because the choppers must often work at close quarters.*

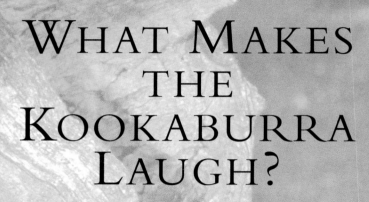

# WHAT MAKES THE KOOKABURRA LAUGH?

By JAMES HUTCHISON

A revealing look at the public and private life
of our gleeful chorister of the bush

*Kookaburra sits in an old gum tree,*
*Merry merry king of the bush is he,*
*Laugh, kookaburra, laugh, kookaburra,*
*Gay your life must be*

As an eight-year-old cub scout in Glasgow, Scotland, I bellowed out the song with the rest of my pack, not having the slightest idea what a kookaburra was. A year later in 1952, my family emigrated to New South Wales, where my first days were spent in wide-eyed wonder at an endless parade of fairy-tale creatures – kangaroos, lizards, huge ants. One morning I was awakened by riotous laughter at my window. Outside a scruffy brownish bird sat in a gnarled gum tree – a kookaburra. It threw back its head and let loose a barrage of raucous laughter. I felt that I had found a merry friend in a new land.

The Laughing Kookaburra is one of ten species of the kingfisher family in Australia and, at roughly 46 centimetres, the world's largest. The bird is indigenous to Australia, yet its scientific name, *Dacelo novaguineae*, mistakenly applied in the 18th century, suggests that the bird comes from New Guinea.

Most kingfishers live near water but Laughing Kookaburras have adapted to open woodlands of eastern and south-eastern Australia. (A similar species, *Dacelo leachii*, the Blue-Winged Kookaburra, lives in northern Australia but does not have a distinctive "laughing" call.) Kookaburras did not exist in Tasmania or Western Australia until successfully introduced there

*Previous page:*
*A hollow in an*
*old gum tree is a*
*favourite nesting*
*place, but almost*
*any flat-bottomed*
*hole of the right*
*size – in a*
*haystack, a wall*
*and even behind*
*the raised letters*
*of a plastic shop*
*sign – will do.*

about the turn of the century. Although some kookaburras were taken to New Zealand in the 1860s, only a small population survives along the western shore of Hauraki Gulf.

The kookaburra's full-throated boisterous laughter is its most famous characteristic. Sounding its call each dawn and dusk, the bird received its onomatopoeic name from the Aborigines. One kookaburra starts with a low chuckle and others soon join in to round out a gleeful but brief chorus.

Generations of Australians have marvelled at the unbird-like call, but none could unlock its hilarious secret. According to Aboriginal legend, the "sky people" called on the kookaburra to awaken them each day so they could light the great fire that illuminates and warms the earth. Tribal law forbade imitating the call for fear of offending the kookaburra and plunging the world into darkness. Early settlers nicknamed the bird "Laughing Jackass" Other colonists, appreciating the

*Research reveals that the kookaburra's ritual laughing at dawn and dusk, in which the entire family joins, is used to mark and reaffirm territorial boundaries.*

early-morning wake-up call, dubbed it the Bushman's clock.

Probably the most famous kookaburra of all was "Jacko," a pet who laughed on command. In the 1930s, he won stage and radio fame, appeared on film and achieved stardom as the kookaburra who cheerfully opened Australian newsreels.

Many Australian suburbanites are familiar with kookaburras arriving regularly on the back veranda for a hand-out of mince, sometimes indignantly tapping a beak on the window if the meal is not delivered promptly.

Kookaburras are fond of snakes, especially young ones to feed to their nestlings, but generally dine on frogs, lizards, worms, spiders, cicadas and grasshoppers. They can spot an insect up to 35 metres away. Lacking sharp talons or a hooked beak, kookaburras depend on their strong neck muscles to help them grip and carry off heavy prey in their bill.

If attacked, kookaburras fight aggressively rather than trying to escape. They spend most of their time staunchly defending their nests and surrounding territory, especially from July to September, the months before the breeding season commences. Termite nests in eucalyptus trees are often pecked and burrowed into cosy hollows. Because their foot muscles are weak, they cannot clamber out of deep holes.

Surprisingly, the social habits of Australia's most famous bird remained obscure until 1965, when Veronica Parry, a young American, began the first scientific study of them for Melbourne's Monash University. Choosing an area at Belgrave in the Dandenongs, Parry set out to unravel the bird's complex social system. "The site was perfect," she says, "the right habitat for our study, plenty of nesting sites, and near the university."

For two years, Parry and her future husband Ernie Madeley poked into the private world of kookaburras, recording the laughs, quarrels and daily activities of 89 birds. Daily during the breeding season, Parry climbed gum trees by rope ladder to check on each nest and its set of one to four small white eggs. Later, she would weigh the growing nestlings. At first, the nesting birds were tolerant, but one day she was struck squarely at the base of her skull by an anxious parent. From then on, she wore a bicycle helmet for protection.

Using a wing-tagging identification system, Parry discovered that, unlike other birds, not all young kookaburras depart the nest to set up their own home. One or more offspring stay home with their parents and forgo mating to help with territory defence as well as the incubation and care of their parents' young the following year.

Since kookaburras live for up to 20 years, have a low death rate and do not all reproduce, this system helps keep their population in check. With Australia's mild winters, there's no need for the birds to migrate. Mating for a lifetime and sometimes occupying the same nest for 15 years, they enjoy a remarkably sophisticated and stable social system.

Despite Veronica Parry's discoveries, no one has done more to introduce this strange bird to the world than Marion Sinclair. As a Girl Guide leader and music teacher, she composed the "Kookaburra" song in 1934, thereby winning a Victorian Girl Guide competition for an Australian round. "I tried koalas, kangaroos, possums and wallabies. I finally gave up," she said from her home in Adelaide. Then one day in the middle of a church sermon, an image of a kookaburra in an old gum tree appeared, and the words and tune sprang to mind.

An instant success, the song was carried home from the big Scout and Guide Jamboree near Frankston, Victoria, in 1934. Today it is sung in more than 100 countries. "Somehow I don't feel the song belongs to me," she said. "Its success was due to a miracle – the miracle of the kookaburra!"

# AUSTRALIA'S ICY ENCHANTRESS

By PAUL RAFFAELE

Few are ever permitted to see Heard Island, one
of the most pristine places on earth

For 11 days out of Hobart, our sturdy little chartered Norwegian research ship *Polar Queen* has battled towering waves whipped up by a roaring, screeching wind. After midnight on the twelfth day, the sea flattens to an eerie calm, and by dawn an icy mist swirls around the ship. On the bridge the mood, usually jocular, is now extremely tense as we near the hidden shoreline of one of the most remote places on earth.

Lieutenant Kevin Slade, a hydrographic surveyor with the Royal Australian Navy, is operating the ship's echo sounder, studying the ocean bottom some 200 metres below. "This area has not been surveyed," he tells me. "For all we know there could be a bloody great rock directly in our path."

At 7 a.m. the mist begins to lift. There before us, hunched beneath a still-hidden 2745-metre volcano, is the shoreline of Heard, part of the only subantarctic island group to escape the ravages of man. All the other islands, like South Georgia, the South Orkneys and Macquarie, are overrun by rabbits, rats and feral cats, their icy slopes host to any number of introduced species of plants.

But Heard Island remains virtually pristine. "It really is a global one-of-a-kind," says Harry Burton, manager of the Australian Government's land-based Antarctic biology program. Heard Island is Australian territory, a 42-kilometre-long stretch of protected sanctuary, which together with 23 other expeditioners I am visiting by special permission of the Federal Government. We don our balaclavas, gloves, long johns, waterproof coveralls and tough caribou boots for the eight hours we'll have on shore.

As the ship drops anchor in Atlas Cove, we stand quietly on deck. To starboard, enormous ice cliffs tower over us, topped

*Previous page: A rare sight, Big Ben is revealed in all its majesty. The fiery heart of the volcano boils and bubbles, but its slopes are cloaked in dazzling snow.*

by steep snow slopes. On the port side, high waves crash against a massive dark rock at the cove's entrance. Then one by one, we inch down a shaky Jacob's ladder, stout twists of hemp connecting narrow wooden slats. Our freezing hands are left ungloved deliberately so that we do not lose the feel of the ropes. Below waits an Australian army LARC, a stubby, orange, 10-tonne amphibious vehicle lowered into the water by crane. As I look down at the pitching vessel, I am painfully aware that on an earlier voyage a woman lost her hold on the ladder and fell into the sea. In the heavy swell she was in grave danger of being crushed between the LARC and the ship. Luckily, one of the crewmen aboard the LARC was able to grab her lifejacket and pull her to safety.

"Time to be moving," says voyage leader Tom Maggs, with a reassuring wink at those of us who now approach our moment of truth. I pause at the bottom of the ladder. "Jump!" shouts one of the LARC crew. His call is timed for the split second when the swell lifts the boat up to the rope. With a silent prayer I throw my ample bulk backwards and land gratefully in the arms of the crew.

As we head for shore, a fierce wind arrives without warning. The LARC surges towards a narrow ice-free isthmus where we are to land. Out on the starboard side, as if on cue, a minke whale rises to the surface, blows up a mighty stream of air and water, then vanishes beneath the surface. A dozen penguins, on the

*Expeditioners on board an amphibious LARC vehicle marvel at the beauty of pristine Heard Island.*

*The gigantic Baudissin Glacier inches its way to the sea between spectacular walls carved out over thousands of years by flowing lava.*

*Above, left, an elephant seal roars his displeasure at intruders on his territory; and right, a nesting gentoo penguin, with its distinctive crimson beak.*

way to offshore feeding grounds, porpoise past us, their sleek black-and-white bodies gleaming in the dark-blue water. Hundreds of giant petrels, sooty albatross and skuas soar over us and shriek into the wind.

About 20 metres out from the beach, the LARC hits the bottom with a heavy bump. Lolling in the shallows are eight massive elephant seals, each some five metres long and weighing as much as a large car. Too clumsy on land to do us harm, they rear up and trumpet their indignation, their long trunk-like noses quivering in disgust.

We wade through the shallows to the beach, a barren stretch of black volcanic sand. On the crest of the beach, 200 metres ahead, is our first destination, the remains of the Australian National Antarctic Research Expeditions (ANARE) base abandoned 35 years ago and now an appalling mess of rusting tractors, rotting planks and discarded oil barrels. The Antarctic Division had given Maggs the task of assessing the damage and organising a cleanup of the area. But our small party can achieve little. "We'll need a bulldozer and a container to clean up and carry all this junk back to Australia," he says.

The derelict base is a tiny blot on an otherwise stunning landscape. Mist, cloud and driving snow still tantalisingly hide Big Ben, the island's volcano – fully visible for only two or three weeks a year. But the ice cliffs fringing the mammoth Baudissin Glacier at its feet are an awesome sight. Formed into high, crenellated walls by thousands of years of lava flows, and iced a shimmering blue-white, they are like the ramparts of a fairytale castle. Below them curves Corinthian Bay, alive with dozens of fur seals bobbing in its milky-blue glacial waters, and thousands of tiny sea birds fishing on its surface.

Close by the remains of the ANARE base, about 50 king penguins honk madly, excited by their first sight of humans. As I approach the rookery, the two biggest kings stride out from the group, thrusting their long beaks into the air as if to impress me with their size. Quickly satisfied that I am not a danger to them, the metre-tall kings swarm around me, peering at the strangest sight of their lives.

Heard Island is home to hundreds of thousands of penguins, including rockhoppers, the red-beaked gentoos and the most numerous of all, the comically punk-looking macaronis. But the largest are the kings. Using depth recorders, scientists have found that kings can dive to a depth of 250 metres. Brought to the very edge of extinction at Heard by 19th-century sealers hungry for meat to supplement their meagre rations, the kings have made a remarkable recovery and are now no longer under threat.

The second LARC has arrived, and the two boats are set up together on the beach to act as a command post. We are restricted to walking around the isthmus, always in sight of the LARCS. "Keep your wits about you all the time," warns Maggs, "because along with all the beauty, this island is very dangerous." In 1952 three expeditioners took a risky short cut at low tide along the beach. They

*A penguin chick waits patiently in the rookery for one of its parents to return with food.*

were hit by a huge wave. One man was swept out to sea and never seen again. The second perished on the glacier while trying to return to the ANARE base for help, while the third man made it safely back. The two who died are remembered by a stark black cross above a moss-covered mound, surely the most desolate grave in the world.

Sobered by the warning, I make my way over to a maze of green marshland behind the penguin rookery, drawn by the snorting and grunting of more than 400 elephant seals. They lie motionless in deep hollows to escape the bitter wind, their huge black, brown and grey bodies like beached torpedoes. More than 45,000 elephant seals return here each year to mate after annual migrations of up to 4000 kilometres.

*Kim Briggs, of the Australian Bureau of Meteorology in Hobart, sets up an automatic weather station on Heard Island. It will relay information crucial to weather forecasting for the southern region.*

Many of the Heard Island elephant seals are marked with red plastic tags. Harry Burton has been tagging their flippers as part of a long-range plan to discover why their numbers are dropping at Heard while remaining constant at South Georgia, a subantarctic island in the Atlantic Ocean.

"It could be related to a rundown in their food supply," he says. East European trawlers regularly fish the waters around the Kerguelen Islands and sometimes come within 200 kilometres of Heard. Burton suspects that over-exploitation or a natural shortage linked to a change in ocean temperatures has robbed these seals of their food supply.

It was the seals that brought the island's earliest explorers. Heard Island was first sighted in 1853 by Captain James Heard while he was sailing from Boston to Melbourne. In the next 30 years, close to 100 voyages, most by American sealing vessels, were made. The early sealers shot or lanced so many elephant seals that by 1880 their numbers had been drastically reduced. Between 1855 and 1880, at least 40,000 barrels of elephant-seal oil were shipped back to America.

This expensive high-grade oil was used for lighting fuel and for many industrial purposes. It was particularly important in cloth manufacturing, where the oil was applied to the wool fibres. Luckily, Heard's fearsome cliffs and crevasses stopped the sealers from working every beach; some seals and penguins survived, and their descendants prospered. On my way back to the ANARE base, I tiptoe past a massive leopard seal sleeping off a penguin-eating binge.

At the base, Kim Briggs of the Australian Bureau of Meteorology in Hobart, clad in a bright-orange weather-proof suit and a Russian-style fur hat, secures an automatic weather station, AWS, to a steel framework on a concrete base. A tall silver cylinder housing a solid state device, it will constantly measure the air temperature and air pressure, employing a VHF trans-

mitter to send the data up to an Argos weather satellite that passes over Heard Island every three hours. "Southern Australia's weather generally moves in from the west," says Briggs, "so information from Heard Island is very significant."

Apart from surveying the old base camp, Maggs is charged with photographing the glaciers at the foot of Big Ben so

*The remains of an Australian research base is a tiny blot on the otherwise pristine landscape.*

Antarctic Division scientists based at the University of Melbourne can monitor environmental changes. The glaciers have steadily been retreating, some very markedly, from the coastline. "Glaciers are sensitive to small changes in temperature," he says, noting that although climate records from Heard are few, other stations in the region indicate that temperatures have risen marginally over the past 40 years. "It could be warming because of the greenhouse effect."

As I make my way back towards the LARC command post at Atlas Cove, a blizzard sweeps with horrifying suddenness from the Antarctic side of the island. One moment the orange LARC is clearly visible about 750 metres across a stretch of black volcanic sand called The Nullarbor. Then a curtain of snow driven by a furious 130-kilometre-per-hour wind envelops me. Quickly donning snow goggles to protect my eyes from the stinging sand, I head off in what I believe is the direction of the LARC.

Minutes later the wind dies down, the snow curtain is raised, and I see the LARC a few hundred metres ahead. Then, just as swiftly, the snow returns on the back of a wind so fierce that I can barely remain upright. For half an hour I criss-cross the sand, terrified that I am losing my way. Then the wind dies down again, the snow stops, and I am safe, only 100 metres from the LARC base.

At 4 p.m. we ride the bucking LARC out to the *Polar Queen* and scramble inelegantly up the Jacob's ladder. As the *Polar Queen* heads out from Atlas Cove, Kim Briggs and I head for the small mess. He is exultant, having just learned from the Melbourne weather bureau that the automatic weather station is transmitting successfully.

I am glum as I eat my meal, frustrated by Big Ben's seemingly inevitable refusal to show itself. But half an hour later,

*The sturdy* Polar Queen, *a Norwegian research vessel chartered for the voyage, is undaunted by the tough conditions in the Antarctic.*

one of the crew manning the bridge phones the mess. "Get up here," he says, "for the sight of your life." We race up on deck. Atlas Cove, rapidly falling back from our stern, is still shrouded in heavy mist. But directly in front of us, the entire sky is deep blue. And framed against it, towering over us, is one of nature's rarest sights: a fully revealed Big Ben, soaring from the ocean, covered from base to summit in dazzling snow.

The volcano is ringed by half a dozen giant buttresses, their edges honed to a brutal sharpness by the unceasing winds. From the crater spirals a thick cloud of steam. The volcano was last active in 1985, and deep within its cone, lava still boils and bubbles, poised for the next eruption.

As the *Polar Queen* heads out to sea, we expeditioners smile broadly and hug one another, drunk with pride that we are among the few who have seen, or ever will see, the beauty that stands before us.

# THE TANTALISING TASTE OF AUSTRALIA

By TONY MAGUIRE

After two centuries of neglect, the native foods
of our continent are back on the menu.

I n a restaurant on Sydney's north shore, marketing representative Warwick Crossman and wife Sue nervously contemplate the dish just set before them: fried witchetty grubs served on a bed of alfalfa sprouts. Gingerly, they pick up two of the plump, cream-coloured moth larvae and, without time for second thoughts, pop them into their mouths. There is a long pause, then Sue declares: "Delicious!"

After two centuries of neglect, our native foods have made the quantum leap from Aboriginal campfires to the tables of fine restaurants. From Sydney to Hobart, Australians are seeking out anything from stewed crocodile to sautéed kangaroo and desserts of succulent berries. "We are being driven by a combination of curiosity, nostalgia for our early days and nationalism awakened by the bicentenary," says botanist Tim Low, author of a book on the wild plants of Australia. "Besides," he adds, "bush food tastes so good."

Before white settlement, Australia's black inhabitants lived off the land in a symbiotic relationship that our modern culture is only just starting to appreciate. Early white explorers, too, made use of the continent's natural food bounty. Native nuts, fruits and vegetables were eaten along with a range of wildlife, from fruit bats to wombats. Sometimes, meals were washed down with an alcoholic brew made from fermented eucalyptus sap. But once transport links were established – and that happened very rapidly – the colonists largely abandoned the labour-intensive bush fare. The Aboriginal diet began to reflect a Western bias, and many of the old hunting and gathering skills were lost.

At an Aboriginal camp 20 kilometres outside Alice Springs, in the country's barren red heart, I join Rod Steinert, an outback tour operator, and a group of culinary adventurers. Steinert gathers us round the dying embers of a campfire, beside

*Previous page: The nutritional content of many of the fruits, nuts and berries that are part of the traditional Aboriginal diet is surprising researchers.*

which sits a diminutive Aboriginal woman. She hands Steinert a length of root and he carefully snaps it in two. "Anyone want to try this?" he asks, fishing out a witchetty grub. The chance to eat a raw, indeed live, moth larva doesn't arise every day. Without further ado, I tuck in. Imagine egg yolk, chicken flesh and almond blended into a liquidy paste and stuffed in a sausage-like membrane, and you'll have a fair idea of what it tastes like.

Next, the woman uncovers a creek frog that has been roasting in the ashes. Steinert divides its body into portions and distributes them for us to nibble at. Like chicken we conclude – albeit a very small chicken. Between nibbles, Steinert declares that his favourite dish is snake. "Carpet snake is my top choice – four or five people can have a really good feed on one. You'd swear you were eating fish," he says. As for other wild meats, he says echidna is a dead ringer for pork and emu isn't far off duck. And kangaroo? "In many ways, kangaroo meat is like lamb."

*An Aboriginal child gets a sweet treat of nectar from native Grevillea flowers.*

For dessert, says Steinert, there is no match for the honey ant. To taste one, I head for the Aboriginal settlement of Papunya. "Just up the road," I'm told. "And while you're there, try to get someone to take you goanna hunting." No bush tucker odyssey can be complete, I am informed, without the thrill of tracking down the legendary giant lizard of the desert.

After a drive some 200 kilometres west along a partly sealed road, I arrive in Papunya. Here I find three grandmothers, Emma Nungurrayi, and her sisters Lurli and Wendy Napanangka, who agree to take me on an ant-foraging party. The women set off into the sparse scrub while grandfather Dinny Nolan Tjampitjinpa and I follow at a more leisurely pace,

*A small group of Aboriginal women out on a food-gathering foray. Men supply the hunted component of the group's diet.*

stopping occasionally to examine an edible plant. Before long, the women spot a few ants and begin excavating around a finger-sized hole in the red earth, searching for a nest. Honey ants gather the sweet secretions of other insects and then re-turn to their own nest to transfer this honey to the specialised ants whose job it is to act as living storehouses.

Following tradition, Tjampitjinpa and I leave the women to their digging and relax under the shade of a mulga tree. Soon, the women are powdered from head to toe with red dust. Emma gives a sudden, exited cry. As we reach her she is with-drawing a stick from a small hole, hooking out a honey ant.

With a grin, she hands it to me. Grasping the two-centi-metre-long ant by the head, I pop the abdomen into my mouth and bite down – and discover that the honey is thinner than the bee-made variety. The liquid runs through my teeth and down my shirt, but I do get a tantalising taste of sweetness offset by a smoky tang. I try a second ant, tilting my head back this time to prevent spillage. Warm nectar floods my tongue.

Back at Papunya we go in search of Ginger Tjakamarra. "Ginger is the one to take you goanna hunting," says Tjampitjinpa. He introduces me to Tjakamarra, a former stockman whose beard is shot with grey and legs bowed from years in the saddle. We set off early next morning and eventually reach a billabong fringed by rocks. There are no animals here now, apart from enormous tadpoles wriggling away in the shallows. We stop for a drink from the billabong before heading on.

Tjakamarra reads animal tracks as an orienteer would a map. "Goanna," he exclaims and points to a row of chevron-shaped marks, like a sergeant's stripes, left behind in the earth by a goanna's clawed feet.

As bare ground gives way to vegetation, Tjakamarra loses the track a couple of times, but quickly finds it again. It's thirsty work and the cool waters of the billabong are now far behind us. Tjakamarra is unconcerned – he simply picks some bush bananas. I follow his lead and bite into the fruit. It's like cucumber but crunchier and more acidic – and very moist. The thirst that was beginning to take hold retreats a comfortable distance. At length we happen upon the entrance to a goanna's lair, a small hole in the red earth. Tjakamarra selects a branch from a mulga tree. He begins jabbing the broken end

*The task of certain ants is to act as storage containers for the honey gathered by other workers. This one's dark abdomen, swollen with nectar to the size of a small grape, yields a delicate taste of honey.*

into the ground a metre or so away from the hole until he finds a spot where it sinks easily into the earth. Getting down on his knees, Tjakamarra digs. "Here he is!"

Suddenly he is pulling a speckled tail out of the ground. The rest of the lizard's body emerges and thrashes violently. The end is mercifully swift. Still holding the metre-long lizard by

*Witchetty grubs are a delicacy to Aboriginal people – they taste like a paste of egg yolk, chicken flesh and ground almond stuffed into a sausage skin.*

the tail, he breaks its neck on the hard earth with a whiplash motion. Next, Tjakamarra trims a length of twig so it has a barb at one end. He plunges the stick into the lizard's throat, working it down to the belly. With a twist of the wrist, he pulls the entrails out through the mouth – less messy than gutting with a knife and the uncut skin conserves moisture during cooking.

Back at his camp, Tjakamarra throws the goanna into a fiercely burning fire. He keeps it there for about three minutes, reaching into the flames with his bare hands every now and then to turn the body. Then he removes it from the fire and waits for the wood to burn away.

When there are only ashes and black embers, Tjakamarra buries the goanna in them. It cooks like that for the next 45 minutes or so. Brushing away ashes from the thickest portion of the body, Tjakamarra prods it with a stick. The skin breaks nicely, exposing succulent-looking white meat. Tjakamarra gives a grunt of satisfaction. "Now we eat," he says.

It's top-quality meat, similar to chicken but denser and oilier. The fire has given it an excellent smoked taste and I gnaw the tail section down to the bone, which I throw to a yellow-eyed dog lurking nearby. Tjakamarra passes me a second piece which I consume with equal gusto.

After a siesta in the shade of the tree, we head back to Papunya. On an earth patch between rocks, Tjakamarra stops and uproots some pea-sized bulbs. "These are *yarlka* – bush onions," he tells me. "Good to eat." Once he has collected ten or so he rubs them briskly between his palms. This removes the dry casing. I try doing the same thing but find that tiny points at the end of each *yarlka* husk dig painfully into my soft city hands. I have to pick off the casing with my fingernails. The *yarlka* tastes slightly hot and slightly sweet, somewhere between an onion and a radish.

Perhaps the best thing to come out of the bush tucker revival is the formal documentation of Aboriginal foods. One of Australia's leading experts on edible pants is an army major, Les Hiddins, who is based at Land Command Battle School in Townsville. Hiddins, who has painstakingly catalogued some 600 edible species, had his first taste of bush food in a Cairns schoolyard. "I used to knock about with Aboriginal kids who'd point out things like green ants and shoots of particular grasses that you could eat," he says.

After two tours of duty in Vietnam, Hiddins took up his search for edible wild plants, convinced that they could one day play a vital role in defence – enabling troops to live off the land while on long-range missions. He was right: his data now forms part of north Australian defence maps. On his first official expedition for the army, south of the Kakadu national

*Cooking the meat of a kangaroo he has killed is a man's job. The technique has been perfected over thousands of years.*

park, Hiddins struck nutritional gold. An old Aboriginal man showed him a tree bearing small green olive-sized fruit. Hiddins sent some off for analysis, photographed the plant and thought nothing more about it until about 1000 kilometres down the track he was found by a policeman and told to call the defence laboratory urgently.

An excited scientist, Keith James, said, "We're getting some extraordinarily high vitamin C readings from that fruit you sent. Can you get some more?" Hiddins drove back across the desert to the same tree – it was only later that he learned that billygoat plum occurs across much of northern Australia. The extra samples he sent confirmed the results – a single billygoat plum has the same vitamin C content as 12 oranges. Horticulturists are now breeding strains for commercial production.

Another native fruit, the quandong, is being grown experimentally by the Commonwealth Scientific and Industrial Research Organisation. Long popular in Broken Hill backyards, where miners prize its tangy flavour, scientists believe the salt-resistant quandong could be grown profitably in areas degraded by salination.

Indigenous nuts are also being tested for their farming potential. The screw palm nut is an ideal high-energy food with a 45 percent fat content. The bush monkey nut, on the other hand, shows promise as a diet nut with a remarkably low fat content of five percent.

The challenge of using this amazing spectrum of foods inspired Jean-Paul Bruneteau and Jennifer Dowling to start Australia's first native food restaurant at Hornsby, north of Sydney. "Bush food provides constant stimulation for a chef," says Bruneteau. "When we started, Australian cuisine was a hotchpotch of European and Asian ideas. I felt that to have a proper national culinary identity our cuisine had to incorporate bush foods," he explains. "Macadamia and bunya nuts were the only Australian food plants I was familiar with when we started out. Now we use about 50 native ingredients."

At Rowntrees, Warwick and Sue Crossman have finished their witchetty grubs and await their next course. Sue has ordered Lamb Podocarpus – loin of lamb stuffed with crushed native pine fruit, while Warwick is having Barramundi Capricorn – filleted fish with a billygoat-plum sauce. In the kitchen, Brun-eteau is adding the final touches.

The culinary pioneering at Rowntrees was the inspiration for other restaurants around the country to start serving bush tucker dishes. Bruneteau and Dowling have been recognised internationally, too. They delighted judges at the Second International Cooking festival in Tokyo with a meal of deli-cacies from the Australian outback. To begin the meal they served an assembly of freshwater croco-dile meat, prawns, Balmain bugs and Tasmanian scal-lops, with a wild finger-lime sauce. Then came water buffalo delicately smoked with banksia cones and garnished with bunya nuts. To round it off there was a pavlova flavoured with wattle seeds. Intrigued, the judges declared it the most original meal of the festival.

Thanks to gastronomic pioneers like Bruneteau and Dowl-ing, the food lore of our continent – so nearly lost for all time – is now being preserved to inspire future generations of Australian chefs. "We've barely scratched the surface," says Vic Cherikoff, a former Sydney nutritional scientist who now cul-tivates bush foods commercially. "There are hundreds of new flavours and textures out there, waiting to delight our palates."

*Westerners have only recently discovered the exciting flavours found in the edible fruits and nuts that grow wild in the outback of Australia.*

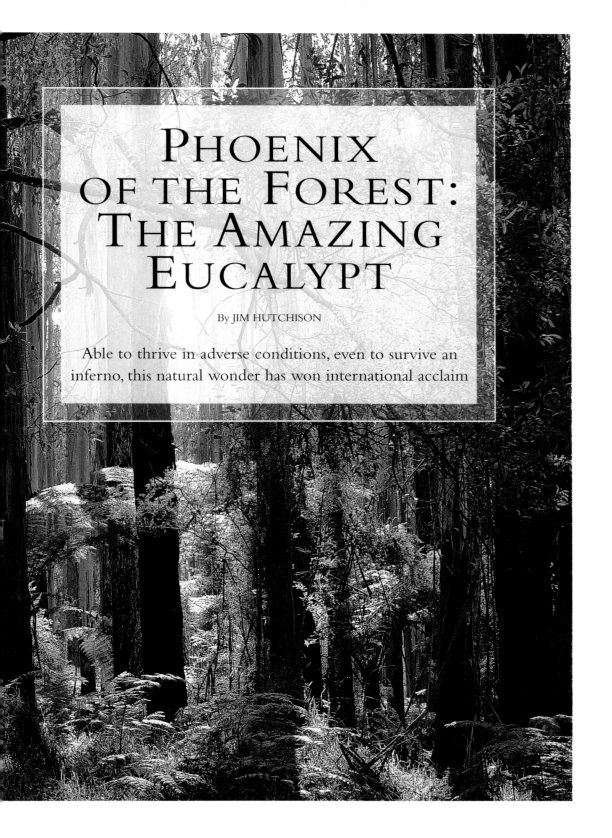

# PHOENIX OF THE FOREST: THE AMAZING EUCALYPT

By JIM HUTCHISON

Able to thrive in adverse conditions, even to survive an inferno, this natural wonder has won international acclaim

M r Liu, my wiry Chinese interpreter, must have seen the black clouds heading towards us. I am now pedalling frantically to keep up with him as he weaves through a stream of straw-hatted farmers on donkey carts and tractors loaded with pigs and vegetables for the markets of nearby Chengdu, capital of Sichuan Province. Clattering into the village, we reach shelter just as the first raindrops soak the dark earth. A pungent, strangely familiar smell suddenly fills the air. "What's wrong?" Mr Liu shouts as I run out into the downpour to stare at end-less rows of eucalypts I hadn't noticed while dodging potholes and people. "They're gum trees," I yell. "From Australia!"

Breathing in the eucalypts' fragrance rising to greet the rain stirs memories of my childhood: flocks of raucous galahs cav-orting in the shaggy crowns of giant river red gums; campfire light dancing eerily over the white trunks of ghost gums; and a kookaburra's mirthful wake-up call from the branches of a gnarled old ironbark outside my bedroom window. Nothing brings Australia more vividly to my mind than the sight and smell of the eucalyptus.

Populating the vast inland deserts and the lush tropical north, even clinging to the high frozen reaches of the Snowy Mountains, these astonishing trees flourish in almost every niche of Australia. On no other continent is a single plant so widespread: 95 per cent of our country's forests are eucalyptus.

Evolved from the myrtle family, eucalyptus is an ancient genus, its pollen first appearing in the fossil record about 34 million years ago. Botanists believe there are as many as 600 different species. Bark can range in colour and texture from the smooth, mottled trunk of the lemon-scented gum, to the thick, fibrous rough brown of the stringybarks. Gumnuts

*Previous page:*
*This forest of*
*mountain ash,*
Eucalyptus reg-
nans, *thrives in*
*central Victoria.*
*This majestic*
*species is the*
*tallest flowering*
*tree on earth.*
*Facing page:*
*Mist drifts among*
*the mountain ash*
*and myrtle*
*beeches of south-*
*eastern Victoria.*

range from ten centimetres across to tiny specimens you can barely see. Although they can live for hundreds of years, most gumtrees do not produce annual growth rings and, to make identification tricky, the leaves and bark of most young eucalypts completely change in appearance as they reach maturity.

When they flower, it is in all the colours of the rainbow except blue.

"Many Australians may be surprised to learn that eucalypts are not really gum trees at all," says Felicity Wishart, a forestry researcher with the Australian Conservation Foundation (ACF). "Sydney's first governor, Arthur Phillip, coined the now popular name in May 1788 for the treacly resin, or kino, that weeps from under damaged bark. It bears no resemblance to true gum, but the nickname stuck anyway." French botanist Charles Louis L'Héritier de Brutelle officially christened the trees "eucalyptus" in 1789, after examining samples collected on Captain James Cook's third voyage. L'Héritier devised the name from two Greek words, *eu* and *kalyptos*, meaning "well covered" – referring to the tough little caps that conceal the trees' blossoms.

*The flowers of Western Australia's lemon-flowered gum,* Eucalyptus woodwardii, *fill the air with a citrus fragrance.*

Since then, gum trees have become inextricably woven into our history and folklore. In the nation's best-known song, the jolly swagman sits under the shade of a coolibah tree – *Eucalyptus microtheca*. Another famous coolibah keeps a lonely vigil out in the arid wilderness at Cooper Creek. Carved on its trunk in 1861, the letters "LXV" can still be seen marking the 65th camp and supply depot of Burke and Wills on their tragic expedition to cross the continent from south to north.

The haunting beauty of Australia's eucalypts has inspired generations of artists and writers. Painter Sir Hans Heysen,

who depicted the great river red gums that line the creek beds and gorges of the Flinders Ranges, wrote of the eucalypt: "Its main appeal to me has been its combination of mightiness and delicacy; mighty in its strength of limb and delicate in the colouring of its covering."

Australian Aborigines have long relied heavily on eucalypts for an inventory of products from spears and totems to cradles and huts. They were producing an antiseptic from gum leaves many thousands of years before eucalyptus oil became a common ingredient in European cure-all potions. Eucalyptus oil is stored in glands that can be seen as tiny transparent dots when the leaves are held up to the light. It has found its way into everything from perfume, disinfectant, mosquito repellent and sheep dip to inhalants and flavouring in confectionery.

Our gum trees' diversity and tenacity have earned them international superstar status. Eucalypts will grow rapidly where no other trees will thrive, even in land with the poorest of soils or most meagre rainfall. Therefore, they are a boon to Third World countries where an estimated 1500 million people depend solely on wood for cooking and heating. Gum trees have almost single-handedly changed the face of Ethiopia, where nearly all the trees are eucalypts.

In more than 100 countries, eucalypts perform a host of worthy tasks. Israel relies on the trees to reclaim brackish swamplands. Vast plantations in South Africa supply a growing demand for construction and paperpulp as well as supports for mine shafts. And in Brazil, on the world's largest eucalypt plantations, up to 900 million gum trees cover the scars of previously clearfelled rainforest.

The bluegums I saw lining the roads in China were planted to combat soil erosion and act as windbreaks. They are part of

*This nocturnal pygmy possum feasting on eucalyptus flowers is just one of the many creatures that rely for food and shelter on the various species of gum indigenous to Australia.*

the "Green Revolution," a massive tree-planting effort aimed at reversing 1000 years of land clearance. The Chinese take their Green Revolution seriously. Officials report that since 1981, under the Public Campaign of Obligatory Tree Planting, some 1000 million trees have been planted each year. At a joint Chinese/Australian reafforestation program in the south, near Nanning, 12,000 hectares of gum trees now thrive.

For two centuries gum trees have been flourishing abroad. I once tried, without success, to convince a California friend that the grand old eucalypts gracing her street were imported a century ago from Australia. "No," she declared adamantly. "They are from California." Tasmanian blue gums have become so much a part of her state's scenery that the trees are known by some as Californian blue gums!

But the ubiquitous gum tree is not without its critics. In

*The hardy gum tree withstands whatever weather nature sends. Here in the Snowy Mountains, in south-eastern Australia, it shrugs off winter snow.*

India, Thailand and Spain, local farmers and environmentalists stormed nursery buildings and uprooted seedlings, saying that the trees are taking over and destroying the landscape.

While many nations flock to plant our gum trees, Australians have been slow to realize their value. "The early settlers saw eucalypts as a curse and cleared them wholesale," says Wishart. "But today, with less than six per cent of our land forested, we ought to know better." Only 12 per cent of our remaining stands are protected in national parks or reserves. In Tasmania, the lofty mountain ash towers nearly 100 metres – the tallest flowering plant on earth. In other countries, trees such as these are revered as tourist attractions. Here, they are in danger of being levelled for newsprint. Says Geoff Law of the ACF, "If Australia's tallest tree were actually cut down and turned into newspaper, the Tasmanian state government would be paid about $280."

Another, more insidious threat to Australia's eucalypts is "dieback," an affliction that sees trees slowly wither from the crown downward. The New England region of New South Wales has already been hard hit: in many places across an area 260 kilometres long and 50 kilometres wide, lifeless skeletons now stand in place of once-thriving gum groves.

"There is a bewildering array of possible causes," explains Dr Ken Old of the Commonwealth Scientific and Industrial Research Organization's (CSIRO) Division of Forest Research. "We just don't have the answer." In Western Australia, a primary cause of dieback is a soil-borne fungus that attacks the roots of jarrahs, but in other areas, causes are more complex.

Preserving gum trees is important not only for humans, but for the survival of a wide range of creatures. Dubbed "nature's boarding house," the tree's basement is alive with insects and borers. On the upper floors, birds nest and rear their young, while koalas and possums nibble the leaftips, and bees arrive when flowers signal feeding time. When a termite-eaten branch breaks off and opens a door into the tree, winged tenants move in: parrots, owls, peregrine falcons, kingfishers, even bats. A third of Australian birds and more than half of all forest mammals depend on old gum tree hollows for nesting.

But perhaps the eucalypt's greatest triumph is its remarkable alliance with fire. Many species have not merely learned to survive the fiery holocausts that sweep the country periodically, but actually welcome them. Some even need the intense heat to reproduce.

Australian gum trees are the worst in the world for spreading fire. With oily leaf litter and twigs accumulating at up to 40 tonnes per hectare, they create their own kindling. When ignited, streamers of peeling bark send flames racing up to the crown, where vaporising oils adds fuel. One of my most frightening experiences was when, as a teenager, I was helping to fight a bushfire in the Adelaide Hills. The fire suddenly started "crowning", then leaping from treetop to treetop. The volatile eucalyptus oil exploded into huge balls of flame, carrying burning bark streamers and branches on hot whirlwinds into other trees kilometres away. In moments, fire was roaring out of control all around us. Eventually, we managed to withdraw to a safe area, but I have never forgotten the terrifying noise and speed with which the fire spread.

*Less than a month after a bushfire, new growth is already sprouting from the base of this badly burned tree.*

Some trees, like the mountain ash, do not survive a fire, but release showers of seeds in the heat, sealed safely in their gumnuts like tiny astronauts in space capsules. (In furnace tests scientists have found that the capsules of some species can protect the seeds for up to four minutes in temperatures of

*The mighty river red gums don't mind getting their feet wet when rivers flood and are greatly valued for the way they can stabilise the river banks.*

400 degrees Celsius.) The seeds scatter onto the rich bed of ashes and are the first to sprout in the new season. But most other eucalypts have an astonishing ability to live through bushfires. Their secret of recovery is a reserve supply of latent buds stored beneath the thick insulating bark in the trunk. Species like the mallee live through the flames and regenerate from bulbous lumps at the base of the trunk called lignotubers.

Not long after the disastrous bushfires of Ash Wednesday, 1983, I visited the small community of Moggs Creek on Victoria's Great Ocean Road. Of 89 homes threatened, only eight survived the inferno. It seemed impossible that the lifeless looking charcoal-blackened trunks, stripped of leaves and branches, could regenerate. But before the first house was re-built, green shoots were miraculously sprouting from the charred trunks. Six years later, there were few signs of the fire amid the lush greenery. One can't help but admire the eucalypt, the Phoenix of the forest, rising undaunted from the ashes. These trees are truly among nature's works of wonder.

# SPIDER! SPIDER!

By TONY MAGUIRE

Watch out…when the world's most fearsome
spider is about

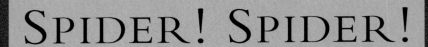

Sydney pharmacist Cam Burnside was drinking coffee in his kitchen one morning when he heard his eight-month-old daughter, Julia, scream. He rushed into the next room and found a golfball-sized spider in the infant's hands. "Julia's been bitten," he shouted to his wife, Wendy. "I think it's a funnel-web!" Burnside called an ambulance while his wife bandaged the child's hands tightly to restrict blood flow.

By the time the ambulance arrived 15 minutes later, Julia's skin had turned bright red, the hairs on her arms were standing on end and she was vomiting. Shortly afterward she was in hospital, breathing in strangled whoops and thrashing her tiny body about. Julia had been bitten by what is probably the world's deadliest spider – the Sydney funnel-web. Its fangs – up to seven millimetres long – can pierce a fingernail or the skull of a lizard, injecting a venom so potent that children who are bitten and go untreated can die within an hour, adults in an agonising two days or more.

"Its venom is one of the most toxic of the 30,000 species of spider in the world," says Philip Lawless, assistant curator of arachnids at the Queensland Museum.

*Previous page: Highly aggressive, the Sydney funnel-web is not a creature to be trifled with. Untreated, its bite can kill a child within an hour or an adult within two days.*

Bite symptoms appear with terrifying speed: within minutes a victim's tongue can go into spasm; there may be nausea, violent retching, sweating and salivation. Breathing becomes laboured, and the victim's muscles writhe like snakes beneath the skin. Meanwhile, acid in the venom may cause agonising pain at the bite site.

The funnel-web's personality is as disagreeable as its bite. Highly aggressive, it will lash out at anything that crosses its path. It can strike again and again, often injecting venom until its reserves are depleted.

Unfortunately, most funnel-webs live in the coastal and highland regions of eastern Australia, the continent's most populous area, and are common in many suburban backyards. Worse, during the summer and autumn mating season, male funnel-webs go on the prowl at night, sometimes wandering into homes. Next day, they shelter from the light under rugs or in shoes or laundry. As a result, many bites occur indoors.

Engineer Peter Melville took a train from his suburban home to his Water Board office in Sydney, where he sat through a two-hour meeting. Afterwards, at his desk, he felt a searing pain in one of his toes. He wrenched off his shoe to reveal a large, black spider.

Rushed to Sydney Hospital, Melville arrived flushed and nauseous, with an irregular heartbeat. Luckily the spider had vented its anger on his shoe leather before finding his toe. By the time it bit Melville, it had all but exhausted its venom supply. Melville was treated and discharged seven hours later. He has since fitted screens to all his doors and windows and thoroughly checks his shoes every morning.

The spider that bit him, *Atrax robustus*, lives solely within a 160-kilometre radius of Sydney, Australia's largest city. "It's one of the deadliest of the 37 funnel-web species," says Dr Mike Gray, a biologist with the Australian Museum. Gray, a veteran arachnologist, has spent years observing the funnel-web in the wild. In a patch of rainforest 50 kilometres north of Sydney, I follow him through a tangle of trees and vines in search of the dreaded spider. Our feet sink into a thick layer of wet mulch. "Ideal funnel-web territory," says Gray.

Suddenly Gray stops beside a rotten log and turns it over with his boot. "Meet the Sydney funnel-web," he says. I glimpse a hairy-legged horror with a chocolate-brown abdomen the size of a cherry and a black thorax and head almost as big again. The outstretched legs would almost cover the top of a soup can. Gray stoops closer, and the spider rears on its hind legs in an attack position. I step backwards. "Don't worry," Gray says with a grin. "Funnel-webs don't jump."

Projecting from below the spider's eyes are a pair of wicked black fangs. "They're as big as the fangs on most snakes," says Gray as he offers a stick to the funnel-web. The spider darts forward, seizing the stick with its front legs and striking with its fangs again and again until Gray shakes it off. Two smears of venom glisten on the wood. The creature scuttles up the log and crawls into the remains of its retreat, a tube of white webbing. The entrance to its lair is often funnel-shaped – the source of the spider's name. It is cleverly sprung with "triplines" running out along the ground. These alert the spider when a potential meal strays within striking distance.

Usually funnel-webs spend their days in nests like these, favouring dark, moist lairs beneath logs, stones or garden debris. They venture out in daylight only when their nests are disturbed by flooding or human activity. When this happens, the numbers can be prodigious.

*The burrow of a funnel-web exposed by a gardener. Favoured nest sites include damp, mulched areas, but they may also wander indoors after a night of hunting and hide in shoes.*

Richard Stubbles, a Sydney pest-controller, was phoned recently by a frantic housewife who said her home was being "invaded" by funnel-webs. Stubbles was sceptical, until he arrived at the house. "It was a nightmare," he says. "There were loads of spiders on the fence and more on the ground." Stubbles spent several hours trying to eradicate the colony, which had been disturbed by a swimming-pool excavation.

*Atrax robustus* has a tree-dwelling country cousin that is less plentiful but just as lethal. Encounters with tree funnel-webs are increasing as more people settle in forested areas of New South Wales. "They're easy to find if you know what to look

for," Gray says, as we pick our way through a paperbark forest near Gosford on the New South Wales central coast. The ground is swampy, and at one point I grab a branch for support. "I wouldn't do that," says Gray. "There are funnel-webs in most of these trees." Soon he points to a spot on the trunk of a paperbark – a mesh of web the size of a hand, camouflaged with bits of bark.

"Watch closely," says Gray, opening a small jar. With a pair of forceps, he picks up a live beetle and touches the insect to the web, which vibrates as the insect struggles. At once the nest bulges, and a pair of multi-jointed legs emerge from a slit a few centimetres away from the wriggling beetle.

*The search for an antivenom took Dr Struan Sutherland more than 13 years of painstaking work.*

The spider rushes forward in a blur and snatches the beetle. Then it scuttles back, dragging its prey into the knothole around which its nest has been built. Putting my ear close to the web, I hear sharp cracking sounds. "Those are the fangs stabbing through the beetle's carapace," Gray explains. Acid in the venom will turn the insect's insides to mush, which the spider will suck out.

By an amazing quirk of nature, most larger animals are immune to the bite – except humans and monkeys, who are highly vulnerable. A dose of funnel-web venom that would have no effect on a dog or cat could kill a person, though scientists are not sure why. One theory is that the structure of primates' receptors allows the poison to attack the nerves very efficiently.

Scientists began seeking an antidote to the venom in the 1920s, but for more than half a century their efforts were thwarted. For one thing, the poison does not behave like snake or redback-spider venoms that block nerve action. Instead, it triggers an overload of electrical impulses to muscles, glands and vital organs. In addition, the venom is hard to obtain in quantity and has little effect on laboratory animals. Snake anti-venom is produced from antibodies in the blood of horses that have gradually developed resistance by being injected with regulated doses of the venom. When the horses were given funnel-web poison, nothing happened. Frustratingly, rabbits produced some antibodies, but not enough to be of any use to humans.

Struan Sutherland, a naval doctor turned immunologist, read a report one day in 1967 about a three-year-old boy who had died within three hours of being bitten by a funnel-web. *That's enough*, thought Sutherland, and vowed to find an antidote.

Working long hours on a shoestring budget at the Commonwealth Serum Laboratories in Melbourne, Sutherland first isolated the venom's active component, atraxotoxin, a concentrated toxin made up of a complex series of amino acids. Then he discovered that mice are vulnerable to the toxin until they are a day old. He began injecting newborn mice with varying doses of venom and blood serum taken from immunised rabbits. But each morning, month after month, the treated mice lay dead in their cages.

The breakthrough finally came one winter morning in 1980. For four months Sutherland had immunised a pair of rabbits with an intensive course of venom injections containing a high concentration of atraxotoxin. He noticed that serum taken from them – carrying a large number of antibodies – had delayed the deaths of one batch of poisoned mice for most of their first day. He wrote in his diary: "By George... a ray of light?" Using protein A-Sepharose, a new antibody-refining material developed overseas, Sutherland then managed to process another batch of rabbit serum to obtain an even higher concentration of active antibodies, something never achieved before.

With growing excitement, Sutherland injected eight new-born mice with venom and antibodies. All survived. Next he gave a laboratory monkey the venom, then administered his antidote to the dying primate a few hours later. When Sutherland left work that night, the monkey was leaping about its cage. *I think I've cracked it*, Sutherland thought.

But he still didn't know if the antidote would work on humans. He flew to Sydney to draw up a protocol with specialists for using it on patients who had no other hope, and left behind a supply of the antidote.

Sutherland didn't have long to wait. One evening in January 1981, Gordon Wheatley, 49, was relaxing in the lounge room of his house in Sydney's northwestern suburbs when a funnel-web bit him on the foot. When he arrived at Royal North Shore Hospital, he was already in a critical condition.

Dr Malcolm Fisher told Wheatley's wife about the new antidote, and she agreed to let him try it. But 15 minutes later, Wheatley's condition was unchanged. In desperation, Fisher rang Sutherland at home in Melbourne.

"Try a second dose," Sutherland suggested. Fisher phoned back 15 minutes later. "It's worked," he said excitedly. Within an hour Wheatley's blood pressure, pulse and pupils had returned to normal. By the end of 1981, the antivenom had saved two more lives and, within months, hospitals across Sydney were requesting stocks of the miracle cure.

Sutherland hopes his creation – one of only four antivenoms developed in the world in the

*Lyn Abra milks her charges of their poison, which will be used to manu-facture the life-saving antivenom.*

## If a Funnel-web Bites You

Medical experts recommend these three potentially life-saving steps:

1. **Apply pressure.** Bandage the bitten limb as firmly as possible to minimise the spread of venom through the body. In the rare 'case of a bite to the trunk or another area that can't be firmly bandaged, try to keep your hand pressed against the punctured skin.

2. **Minimise movement.** Exertion speeds up the spread of the venom, so it is essential you remain as still as possible. Call others to help you. If the bite is on an arm or a leg, immobilise the limb with a splint.

3. **Get to hospital.** If possible, have someone phone ahead to let staff know you're on your way. Do not remove pressure bandages until antivenom and resuscitation equipment are at hand.

past three decades – may serve as a model in other types of therapy, including cancer treatment. "In theory, the same immunisation method can be used to create antibodies that attack tumours," he says.

The donors for Australia's antivenom program are some 300 male *Atrax robustus* spiders kept at the Australian Reptile Park in Gosford. These are "milked" every week by their keeper, Lyn Abra. "We keep them in darkness," she says, drawing back black curtains along one wall of her laboratory to reveal shelves stocked with dozens of glass jars. She places one on a workbench and unscrews the lid.

At the base is a five-centimetre-thick layer of potting mix carpeted with frost-white web. In a small depression to one side lurks a big spider. Abra picks up a pair of forceps and gently nudges the spider with them. It rears, exposing clusters of fiery, reddish-brown hairs on the underside of its body. At the end of each fang, I clearly see a droplet of venom.

Abra touches the end of a pipette – a long, thin tube of siliconised glass connected to a vacuum pump – to the left fang and sucks away the droplet. The spider strikes at the instrument, its fangs tapping audibly against the glass.

Unperturbed, Abra deftly milks the other fang. She repeats the process, which takes less than ten seconds, to ensure she has all the venom. After Abra has milked all her charges, she uses a weak acetic-acid solution to flush the contents of the pipette into a glass vial, and stores the liquid venom in a freezer. It will be packed in dry ice and air-freighted to the Commonwealth Serum Laboratories in Melbourne. There it will be injected into rabbits to develop fresh batches of antivenom for distribution to hospitals, ready to treat the funnel-web's next victims.

At the Accident and Emergency Department of Hornsby Hospital, Julia Burnside lay unconscious, her infant body drenched with sweat. An hour had passed since her parents had discovered the funnel-web in her hands. Her mother, Wendy, sat by her bed, listening to the hiss of the machine that was breathing for her baby. Please God, she prayed, don't let her die. Registrar Dr Garry Browne had already given Julia several doses of the antivenom, but with no measurable improvement.

He was deeply concerned. No child had ever been given such large doses of antivenom. But Julia's blood pressure was dangerously high at 127/104, and her pulse was racing at 200 beats a minute. Browne decided to risk another dose. He injected the liquid into the intravenous line in Julia's arm and waited, anxiously scanning the blood–pressure monitor above the bed. Suddenly he smiled. "It's coming down!"

By 8 p.m. Julia's blood pressure was almost normal. She opened her eyes and looked at her parents, then held out her arms to be picked up. "Welcome back, sweetheart," Wendy said, tears of joy running down her cheeks.

A week later, with Julia back to normal, Wendy phoned Struan Sutherland at his laboratory. "Without you, Julia would not be here," she said. "Thank you for saving our little girl."

*Little Julia Burnside owes her life to Dr Struan Sutherland's determination to find an antidote to the venom of the deadly funnel-web spider.*

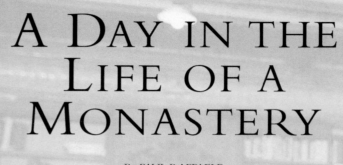

# A Day in the Life of a Monastery

By PAUL RAFFAELE

Behind the high walls of this Australian religious
community, there is hard work, ceaseless prayer —
and just a hint of devilment

5 a.m. An hour before dawn, a church bell's clanging wakes the monks of New Norcia monastery in the Australian countryside 130 kilometres northeast of Perth. In his cell, Dom Placid Spearritt, the monastery's prior, dons a heavy black cowl, pulling the high, pointed hood over his head to ward off the chill. His 11,005th day as a Benedictine monk will begin with Vigils, the first of seven daily periods of communal prayer.

5:15 a.m. In the chapel, before an ornate Spanish altar, 25 monks stand motionless in their carved pews, hands tucked under their cowls, linked in a ritual that has barely changed since St Benedict of Norcia, Italy, wrote his Rule, regulations for monastic life and discipline, 1500 years ago. As they chant the words of the 27th psalm, their voices mingle with the dawn stirrings of parrots and kookaburras in the eucalyptus trees surrounding the brown-and-white stucco monastery building.

New Norcia was founded by Dom Rosendo Salvado and Dom Joseph Serra, Spanish monks who journeyed here from Italy in 1846 intent on converting the Aborigines. Gradually, over the next three decades, Salvado established a monastery, recruiting 80 monks from Spain and Italy. Skilled in the classical arts, they also readily bent their backs to building, ploughing, turning the flour mill and the olive press.

5:40 a.m. The monks leave the chapel for their cells and a period of quiet contemplation before breakfast and more prayer. Dom Placid's cell, like the 30 others that ring the second and third floors of the building, is a small room with a narrow bed, writing desk and a cupboard holding his two winter black robes and two summer white robes. Like all Benedictine monks, Dom Placid owns nothing, not even his spectacles. "We are only allotted property for our use, such as a watch," he explains.

*Previous page: A monk at work in the monastery library, which houses some 40,000 books, more than 1000 of them dating from before 1800.*

*Opposite: New Norcia's Abbey church has a distinctly Spanish character.*

*Through the elegant gates of the monastery visitors catch a glimpse of the peaceful garden.*

7 a.m. After joining the other monks in the refectory for breakfast, Dom Placid returns to the office that adjoins his cell to confront a pile of paperwork. Often among his daily correspondence are letters from young men who want to join the order. "There's no shortage of would-be recruits," says Dom Placid. But very few applicants succeed — the first in seven years joined them as a novice last year. "I immediately suspect that men who say they are disgusted with the modern world are running away from something," he adds. "You do not escape from the world by coming to a monastery."

7:30 a.m. Dom Placid is interrupted by the church bell that tolls every 15 minutes, day and night, decreeing how every moment is spent. It is time for Mass, the third prayer period of the day. For this, the monks file silently through the monastery's iron gates to the Abbey church beyond. "For some of the monks, it's probably the only journey they will make outside the walls all year," says Dom Francis Byrne, a lively Irishman who once dodged army bullets and teargas canisters as a journalist in Belfast.

On the way to his pew Dom Francis rests his gaze on a painting of the Madonna and Child given to Salvado by St Vincent Pallotti in Rome in 1845. Some of the monks claim it is miraculous. In 1847 a massive bush fire swept towards the infant monastery and its crops. "Our hands and faces were burnt, our beards singed and our habits scorched," Dom Salvado despaired, "for the flames were high against us." In a desperate gesture, Dom Salvado took the picture and placed it against the nearest stalks of wheat, which seemed ready to catch fire. "No sooner was the sacred image of Mary placed in front of the fire," he marvelled, "than the wind blew in the opposite direction, carrying the flames away."

8:30 a.m. Dom Paulino Gutierrez is already hard at work in one of the monastery's farm sheds, operating the diesel olive crusher. The monastery's 300 olive trees produce some 570 litres of oil each year. "I like hard work," says Dom Paulino, who toils seven days a week. "It makes the time pass more interestingly." Over the past 63 years his duties have included milling the monastery flour, baking bread, nursing sick colleagues and serving as monastery bootmaker. He gently teases the other monks about their modern 16-hour day. "Until 20 years ago, we rose at 4 a.m. and prayed four or five times as much as now, while doing the same amount of work," he says. "We had to do it all on eight ounces of food at the main meal, strictly weighed."

11 a.m. Dom Christopher Power, tall, bearded, soft-spoken, is talking into a two-way radio in his office. He is the Procurator (a Latin term for business manager) and is also responsible for the smooth functioning of the town and the welfare of the

*Commencing with Vigils at 5:15 a.m., the monks gather for communal prayer seven times a day. The last office is Compline, sung at 8:10 p.m.*

monastery's 50 employees. He phones Keith Hunt, a professional farm manager who is harvesting the monastery's 1400 hectares of wheat. "We should start in a couple more days and finish within six weeks," Hunt tells him.

"Most people expect us to be out in the fields driving oxen behind the plough," Dom Christopher says with a smile, "but we use the most modern farm machinery. The Bible enjoins us to be good stewards, and technology helps us to achieve that."

Half of New Norcia's 8000 hectares is farmland that includes grazing for some 70 cattle and 13,000 sheep. The remainder is fenced-off bushland where kangaroos, emus and a wealth of birdlife live in peace. "We have a strong lobby for

*The monastery farm employs about 50 people apart from the monks. It produces wheat, cattle and sheep, as well as vegetables and fruits for the table.*

conservation among the monks," explains Dom Christopher.

11:30 a.m. In the monastery library the records of the 40,000 books are being updated. "There are more than 1000 titles that predate 1800," sub-prior Dom David Barry says proudly. "It's one of the most significant libraries in Western Australia." A man of varied talents, Dom David speaks French, Spanish, Italian and some German and Hebrew. Once he spent two years as a jackeroo, riding herd on cattle in bush camps in the outback.

Noon. A bell summons Dom Francis and his fellow monks to chapel for the day's fourth round of prayers. Unlike most of the others, he doesn't wear a watch and relies entirely on the bell for the time. "The hardest is to wake up at 5 a.m. for Vigils," he says, "but Dom Seraphim alerts me by ringing the prayer bell." Normally, the 78-year-old Dom Seraphim Sanz gets it right, but one morning he misread the time and rang the bell at 2 a.m. "I scampered down to the chapel," says Dom Francis. "The lights were off, and I said to myself, *They're finished, everyone is gone, I'm late again.* I checked the kitchen clock and saw that it was just 2 a.m. I started cursing Dom Seraphim before I begged the Lord's forgiveness and went back to bed."

After prayers, the monks file silently into the refectory, a narrow hall lined on either side with long, dark wooden tables. Lunch is chunky chicken soup, fragrant lamb chops from monastery sheep, peas, sweetcorn and mashed potatoes, followed by peaches smothered with thick fresh cream. "Good food is good for the monks' morale," says Dom Placid.

The men are forbidden to speak during meal times. There is just the steady, amplified drone of Dom Anthony Lovis reading first from the Bible, then from a secular work such

*Dom Paulino enjoys turning his hand to the daily tasks the monks must carry out but maintains that the monks now lead easier lives than in former times.*

as a history or biography. Dom Placid explains that the rule of silence enables the monks to concentrate on the readings. "St Benedict says that at meal times we should feed the soul as well as the body."

1:30 p.m. As the other monks head for their cells for their daily one-hour siesta, Dom Placid strolls through the monastery's garden with Dom John Erickson, a visiting monk from the United States' first Benedictine monastery, St Vincent's, outside Pittsburgh. "We have cafeteria Benedictinism," says

Dom John wryly. "Meals are served at a stand-up buffet because we're on the go all the time." He says he has been moved
to take his lunch in the serene way Benedictine monks have
for 1500 years. "If I were young, I would want very much to
spend my life here at New Norcia."

3:05 p.m. One of New Norcia's most senior monks, Dom
Bernard Rooney, is heading back to New Norcia from Moora,
50 kilometres to the north. There, he spends three days a week
teaching Aborigines the traditional dances, customs and language often forgotten since the white man arrived 160 years
ago. Dom Bernard, who is in constant contact with people
outside the monastery's walls, is often questioned about the
relevance of his lifestyle in the modern world, especially the
monks' vow of celibacy.

"A local mayor once told me, 'I don't understand how you
monks can live without a woman.'" Dom Bernard grins with
just a hint of devilment. "Imagine this monastery with 25
women and probably twice as many kids. It would be bedlam.
Our life of work and prayer would be impossible."

Other centuries-old traditions have been discarded. "When
I was a novice, three decades ago," says Dom Bernard, "we
heard tales of a Novice Master who would walk up and down
the corridor listening as the novices beat themselves with
whips in their cells for penance." These days a penance is a
bread-and-cheese supper on Friday nights. "And that's not
much of a sacrifice," he adds. "The monastery serves an excellent spread of cheeses."

4:45 p.m. Dom Francis walks towards the small guesthouse
adjoining the monastery. It houses visitors who come from all
over the country for retreats, and he is the monastery's Guest
Master. This afternoon he reads from one of the books of con-
templative poems he has had published. A guest raises the most

common question Dom Francis is asked: Why did he, a much-travelled journalist named Frank Byrne, opt for such an unlikely life?

"I think it was Socrates who said that the unreflected life is not worth living," Dom Francis replies. "More than ever before, there is a great need for people to find quiet places like New Norcia where they can pray and recollect themselves."

5:30 p.m. Dom Francis returns to his cell, slips into his jogging gear and puffs his way along a deserted bushland track. "The food is so good here," he says, "that unless I jogged most days, I'd look like Friar Tuck."

7 p.m. Following the chanting of Vespers in the chapel, the monks are served plump, homemade sausages spiced with herbs and floating in a rich tomato stew, followed by fresh fruit. The meal ends with Dom Anthony reading the names of some of the Benedictine monks, from monasteries worldwide, who have died on this day over the past century.

7:30 p.m. Most of the monks cross the cloister to the recreation room. Some watch the news, one of the few TV programs permitted, along with documentaries and cricket. Others scour today's edition of *The Australian* or settle back with a current-affairs magazine.

8:10 p.m. The monks climb the stairs to the chapel for the day's final prayers, Compline. They sing the song of the old priest Simeon, *Nunc dimitis servum tuum Domine, secundum verbum tuum in pace* – Now, Lord, let your servant go in peace, according to your word. After Compline, the monks return to their cells, where the Magnum Silentium, or Great Silence, takes effect. Some monks will continue reading, while others will pray.

10 p.m. As the bell clangs the hour, Dom Placid kneels before his bed, seeking inspiration in his efforts to build a

secure future for New Norcia. He reflects on a remark by Dom John earlier in the day: "There are many in America who yearn for stable communities like ours, where men are willing to give up everything for the great values of life."

Dom Placid hangs up his habit, smiling with renewed optimism. He climbs into his pyjamas, lowers his head to his pillow and, almost instantly, falls asleep. It is the deep, calm sleep of a man who has lived the day to its fullest.

*A sense of peace pervades the beautifully decorated interior of the monastery.*

# RIDING THE ROAD TRAIN

By PAUL RAFFAELE

Climb aboard for an outback adventure on one of the
world's most remarkable vehicles

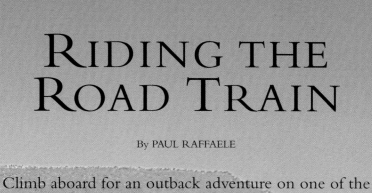

I t's noon and a heat-haze flows like quicksilver over the dirt road between Kununurra and Timber Creek in Australia's Top End. A faint breeze stirring the clumps of dry grass carries the hum of a distant engine. Soon the corrugated surface begins to tremble with the pummelling of heavy wheels. Then, round a bend in the road, a monster truck heaves into view, its chrome exhaust stacks bellowing. Behind a giant cab rolls a trailer almost as long as a railway goods van and nearly five metres high. Behind that thunders a second massive trailer. Then, impossibly, comes a third trailer, as tall and as long as the others.

A road train! These leviathans of the outback are the biggest general freight-carrying vehicles in the world, roaming over a million square kilometres of Australia, bringing food, fuel and the necessities of life to the outback population. "Road trains are our lifeline," says former Northern Territory Chief Minister Marshall Perron. "They make life in the territory possible."

The only rivals to Australia's road trains are the 35-metre double-trailer trucks permitted in several US states. But in Australia, where traffic is sparse, road trains can stretch more than half the length of a football field. Driving them takes extraordinary skill: "Imagine driving a car with three caravans attached," says Ian Berryman, operations manager for the Katherine-based Road Trains of Australia, "then multiply the weight about 30 times."

But even among this trucking elite there is a still more exclusive group: the cattle-train drivers. These men pilot two-storey rigs that carry 150 beasts at a time and travel on narrow dirt roads tough enough to test a four-wheel drive.

Undisputed king among these men is Noel Tones, a deeply tanned 49-year-old with brown eyes and a handshake like a wheel clamp. "Tonesy's the best in the territory," I was told

*Previous page: Three double-decker trailers, each loaded with cattle, barrel along behind the prime mover. It takes extraordinary skill and courage to handle these monster road trains.*

time and again by road-train veterans. I arrange to ride with Tonesy, who works out of Katherine, from Newry cattle station where he is due to take on 150 head of cattle for an 88-kilometre trip to Darwin.

His road train is a one-man traffic jam: a shining green-and-white 14-litre Kenworth prime mover hitched to three double-decker trailers, each deck divided into two compartments that hold 12 or 13 cattle. From its bull bars to the tail lights of the rear trailer the vehicle measures 50 metres. Others can go up to 53.5 metres. "That's the maximum allowed," says Tonesy, as bellowing cattle mill about the yard, kicking up clouds of red dust.

Swarms of bush flies attack us, covering our clothes, buzzing about our eyes and mouth. Four cowhands wave their hats and yell as they herd the cattle up a ramp to the top deck. Tonesy whoops and hollers, slamming the gate shut when 12 bulls fill the first of the compartments. "You've got to know cattle in this job," he smiles.

*It's the driver's responsibility to deliver the 150 beasts in a typical shipment in good condition. Tonesy watches closely as the cattle in his care are loaded.*

It takes about two hours to load all the beasts and Tonesy runs his expert eye over every cow and bull coming aboard. He's responsible for getting them safely to their destination. "That means I can refuse to take any I think are lame or sick."

With the last of the cattle loaded, Tonesy grabs an iron bar and bangs it on each of the rig's 62 tyres, seeking any that are under-inflated. On each the bar bounces back with a healthy *boing*. "Now we're ready," he says.

The Kenworth is as high as a suburban house and I have to climb a built-in ladder to get in. The twin exhausts belch black smoke as Tonesy twists the ignition key and the turbo-charged

*The cattle are urged up a ramp into the upper and lower decks of each trailer. They are packed in tightly enough that they support each other.*

engine chatters into life. For a full minute we sit motionless as the engine's air compressor builds up pressure in the air brakes. Then Tonesy dabs the brake pedal and there is an answering hiss from the multiple air-brake systems: one for each set of wheels. He shifts the gear stick and the rig creeps forward, smoothly taking up its 115-tonne load. We're off!

I feel a surge of boyish delight as we head down the road. At Newry's main gate, Tonesy swings into a wide, careful turn. "If you turn too hard or too fast," he explains, "the rig can jackknife and crush the cab. It's happened." I look back anxiously but the trailers are following dutifully, nose to tail like circus elephants.

The Kenworth generates almost 400 kilowatts of power, but the inertia of the payload is so massive that Tonesy has to work laboriously through all 18 gears to reach cruising speed of 85 km/h. As we thunder along the dirt road, I see his eye flick constantly to the huge rear-view mirrors flanking the cab. The rearmost trailer is hidden by dust. How will he know if something is wrong? "If the trailers start wandering off course, I can feel the sway in the cab," he says.

The locals show us great respect. Up ahead, a dust-spattered Landcruiser sees the Kenworth barrelling down the road and immediately pulls over to the side. Tonesy gives the driver a thank-you wave as he passes. "Sensible bloke," he observes.

I can hear the cattle bellowing as we drive. "They've never been in a truck before," says Tonesy. "But they'll get used to it after an hour or so – once they've found their feet."

We reach an unmarked crossroads but Tonesy steers confidently to the left. "Got to know your way on a road train," he says. "You can't reverse or do a U-turn." Inevitably, learner drivers get it wrong sometimes. That means unhitching the trailers and dragging them round one by one before connecting them up again.

"Something's up," says Tonesy and quickly lifts his foot from the accelerator. He points ahead to a dark object on the side of the road. As we slow I see it's a calf, lying on its side, legs moving weakly. "It's been hit bad by a car. Shoulder's smashed, poor little bloke." He decides to wait for someone who can take the calf to Newry but it's 15 minutes before a truck passes. "He may have to be put down," says Tonesy as we place the calf in the back, "but at least he won't die slowly in the sun."

Back on the road, we encounter a series of creeks crossed by single-lane bridges barely a handspan wider than the truck on either side. Tonesy's skill in steering over them is astonishing. "With experience, you do it by instinct," he says as we zoom across one at 70 km/h. Despite their skill, however, road-train drivers have an average of one accident a year,

*Noel Tones, the undisputed king of an elite group who handle these giant cattle transporters on the highways.*

mostly collisions with stray cattle or minor bumps in small towns. Occasionally drivers pay a higher price. As we cross bone-dry Skull Creek, Tonesy spares a thought for a friend who crashed into the riverbank, killing himself instantly. "His truck was named Whispering Death," he says.

What will happen if we meet a road train like ours coming the other way? Half an hour later I get my answer: a massive green three-trailer Mack truck is barrelling towards us. Tonesy's Kenworth already takes up most of the road. My eyes widen as the other truck nears. Neither vehicle slows. We're going to hit! At the last moment the two drivers steer their outside wheels onto loose dirt, performing a neat *pas de deux* that throws up a storm of red dust.

We're so close I can see the stubble on the other driver's face. A sign on the road train's side reveals that it's from Perth, 3000 kilometres away. "He's been carting vegetables to Darwin," says Tonesy. "Most road trains from Perth travel round the clock, with two drivers rotating the work-load." He scorns the predictable life of the freight road trains, hauling groceries, fuel and other essentials from settlement to settlement. "That would drive me mad."

Road-train drivers have always been a hardy breed. After World War II, new settlers poured into the north, populating mining camps and cattle stations as the demand for beef grew. With such a scattered population in a vast area, the territory could not sustain an extensive railway system to carry cattle to the market. The surplus of ex-army gear around after the war meant that men like Kurt Johannsen, a jack-of-all-trades living in Alice Springs, could use old tanks and Bren gun carriers to fashion vehicles suitable for transporting cattle. These powerful, manoeuvrable prime movers with self-tracking trailers could cope with the rigours of Northern Territory roads without damaging the cattle.

Before the war, drovers on horseback took around five months to drive cattle 1500 kilometres and the stock often arrived in poor shape. But Johannsen's new road trains could get them to market faster and in better condition. Within a few years, the drovers were largely gone.

As we head along a narrow stretch of dirt road a few kilometres west of Victoria River, a camper van comes over a rise, hogging the road. Tourists often aren't familiar with road trains and Tonesy gives a warning tug on his air horn. The sharp blast has no effect.

"What the heck does he want me to do?" mutters Tonesy. His eyes search for an escape route, but sturdy gum trees line the road and it takes up to half a kilometre to stop the rig.

Now we're only 30 metres apart. Tonesy curses, preparing to floor the brake pedal. He knows that locking the wheels in an emergency stop will strip the treads and cost thousands of dollars. Suddenly the camper van is yanked over to the left. The Kenworth rushes past, showering it with pebbles and missing it by just a few centimetres. "Bloody hell," says Tonesy.

By noon we reach a Timber Creek roadhouse with tin-roofed restaurant and service station. Tonesy checks the animals, then we go in and order a Hamburger With The Lot. As we eat, Tonesy tells me about his childhood on a cattle station like Newry. "My dad claims I fell in love with the smell of diesel at the age of four," he says.

We emerge, blinking into the sunlight. The temperature is hovering around 40 degrees but the rig is air conditioned, built to handle the outback's searing heat. "Until I got a modern rig ten years ago," Tonesy says, "I sometimes had to line the floor of the cabin with wet sacks to dampen the heat from the sun and the engine."

Tonesy can relax a little on the main highway to Katherine. He has two radios in his cab: a standard UHF radio for talking to other truckies, and a shortwave radio to call his base in Katherine. He thumbs a switch on the shortwave and it crackles to life. "Base, this is Tonesy," he says. "I'm at Willaroo. I'll be there in a couple of hours."

Even now, with a good surface, Tonesy can't relax completely. Going down a steep hill he can feel that the rear trailers are starting to "snake". He eases up on the accelerator and lets the rig coast while pulling a lever on the steering column that allows him to operate the brakes on the trailers independently of the prime mover. The pull of the Kenworth against the drag of the trailers draws the train back into line.

Tonesy glances at his watch. It's two hours since our last stop and, in an unfailing ritual, he pulls the Kenworth to a halt. Making a circuit of the road train, he bangs each tyre with the iron bar, and sniffs the air for any sign that the wheel bearings or brake linings are getting hot. All's well. Out here in the bush Tonesy is extra careful. He's had to pull back in a hurry plenty of times after spying a deadly king brown snake or a desert death adder coiled round the axle. "They like sleeping on the road," he says, "and they get whipped by up by the wheel."

By 4 p.m. we are nearing Katherine, still 400 kilometres from Darwin but home to Tonesy and his wife, Gwen. "Let's give her a surprise," he says, grinning, as we rumble up to their tin-roofed bungalow.

But the stopover can last only an hour. Tonesy's three-year-old camel, Candy, walks gawkily across the paddock and greets him by nuzzling his neck. "Her mother died at a remote settlement when Candy was a baby," he says. "The local store owner phoned me and asked if I wanted her because she wasn't being properly looked after."

While Tonesy has a shower I discover that the eight-hectare property is full of animals he has rescued. A dozen calves gambol about the paddock, all once under threat of death

*Gwen Tones pets Candy, a young orphaned camel who is now part of the Tones household's menagerie of rescued animals.*

because their mothers had perished about loading time. Sometimes they get injured by stampeding cows. "Tonesy brings them home and we have a vet fix them up," explains Gwen.

There's time for a cup of tea and then we drive the seven kilometres to Tonesy's base in Katherine, from which Road Trains of Australia operates a fleet of 20 of these monsters. Here Tonesy unhitches the trailers, then edges the prime mover up to a diesel pump.

With 1800 litres of fuel on board, we set off again. Evening is drawing in and I start to doze off, lulled by the rumble of the engine. Suddenly I'm woken by a loud bang. Tonesy eases down the brake pedal. "Bloody tyre," he says climbing down from the cabin. An outer tyre on the second trailer has blown and hangs in tatters round the rim. He hauls out a large jack, four times the size of a car jack and capable of lifting 20 tonnes, and begins to fit one of the rig's 12 spare tyres.

For more than an hour we've been approaching a big bushfire sparked by lightning strikes on dry grass. Its red glow illuminates the night sky. I expect Tonesy to turn away, seeking an alternative route, but he keeps on driving. Flames tower into the sky on both sides of the road. Silhouetted by the eerie glow, scores of black kites dive about the sky chasing swarms of insects fleeing the flames. Tonesy drives on unconcerned, having passed through more bushfires than he can remember. "It's just a local flare-up – we'll be out of it soon," he assures me.

By 11 p.m., Tonesy has had enough. He pulls over into a rest area. Many drivers have televisions and videos set up in their bunks to while away the 200 or more nights they spend each year on the road, but Tonesy is made of sterner stuff. He either drives or sleeps.

At first light the next morning we stir, woken by hundreds of pink and grey galahs that swirl around in the clear sky before flying off to their feeding grounds. Tonesy checks the cattle, then heats a cup of coffee on a gas burner before performing his ritual tyre banging.

The small trees and shrubs of the semidesert have given way to palms and spiky pandanus plants. From our overnight stopping point it's only three hours to Darwin. How on earth will Tonesy pilot the Kenworth through city streets? The answer, I soon discover, is very carefully. Far below us, drivers glance nervously in their rear-view mirrors as they hear the stuttering hiss of compressed air from our brake units. Tonesy has to stay constantly alert. "I'm watching about six cars ahead all the time," he explains. "That way I gain extra braking time."

We make it through the city unscathed. A Malaysian live-cattle transport ship, the *Brahman Express*, is waiting at the dockside. Tonesy opens the gates and the cattle are driven up a ramp to the ship. Then he drops the trailers at a local depot and, free of it's train, he drives the Kenworth to a motel.

"Time for a coldie," he calls.

We sit in his room, beers in hand, swatting mosquitoes. But after his marathon drive, one can is enough for Tonesy. "Time for some shuteye," he says. Tomorrow he'll be back in his train. "It's a short trip this time," he says with a smile. "Less than 2000 kilometres to Broome."

THE LIBRARY WITHDRAWN COLLEGE SWINDON